ADDITIONAL PRAISE FOR
MAKING LIFE LESS TAXING

"Kim Moody lays out in plain English the complexities of the Canadian tax system with frankness and zeal while debunking common tax myths. His in-depth tax knowledge is showcased throughout the book as he philosophizes on tax, explores recent tax history, and suggests possible tax solutions within the context of our current world. I recommend this book for any small business owner, entrepreneur, cross-border business, or Canadian who wants the quintessential road map to Canadian tax."
  –Jay Goodis, CPA, CA and Co-Founder and CEO, Tax Templates Inc.

"The beauty of this book is the simplicity of the message on a topic that can be so daunting and complex. As a business owner, you don't know what you don't know–this book will open your eyes."
  –Amish Morjaria, Founder + CEO, Forward Level Marketing

"I have known Kim, both personally and professionally, for over 20 years. In the financial planning world, collaboration is key, and most often, we work with accountants to maximize financial outcomes for our clients. In the times Kim and I have crossed paths, his tax advice and input has been exceptional and I can say without hesitation that Kim Moody is one of Canada's leading authorities on matters pertaining to tax. Further, what really sets Kim apart is not only his ability to provide leading edge tax advice, but to do so, in an understandable and straightforward manner. Anyone who has significant wealth, would be well advised to listen to what Kim has to say."
  –Brent Peacock, co-founder and partner of the Peacock Sheridan Group

"Kim is one of the strongest private company tax specialists I've known in my own career as a tax specialist. He lives and breathes tax and he questions the status quo. Let's face it, someone who has chaired the Canadian Tax Foundation, The Joint Committee of the Canadian Bar Association and CPA Canada and the Society of Trust and Estate Practitioners is someone you can learn from."
  –Peter Weissman, FCPA, FCA, TEP and Partner, Cadesky Tax

MAKING LIFE LESS TAXING

MAKING LIFE LESS TAXING

PAY ATTENTION TO YOUR TAXES SO YOU CAN PAY LESS
TAX AND BUILD A STRONGER, SMARTER CANADA

KIM G C MOODY

Redwood Publishing, LLC
Ladera Ranch, CA
info@redwooddigitalpublishing.com

Printed in Canada and the United States of America.
First Printing, 2020.

ISBN: 978-1-952106-26-2 (paperback)
ISBN: 978-1-952106-27-9 (ebook)

Library of Congress Cataloguing Number: 2020904189

Interior Design: Jose Pepito
Cover Design: romy

Disclaimer: This book is designed to provide information and motivation to its readers. It is sold with the understanding that the author and publisher are not engaged to render any type of psychological, legal, or any other kind of professional advice. The content of each article is the sole expression and opinion of its author and is not meant to substitute for any advice from your healthcare professionals, lawyers, therapists, business advisors/partners, or personal connections.

First Edition
10 9 8 7 6 5 4 3 2 1

CONTENTS

My wife—Vivian. Your unwavering support and being an unbelievable Mom to our sons has been a continuing inspiration to always do my best...I love you!;

My 4 sons—you will likely never know how much you mean to me...and thanks for laughing at my "Dad jokes"!;

My business partners—Paul Lebreux, Dale Franko, Kenneth Keung, and Alexander Marino—thanks for Transforming Tax Services by Making Complexity Irrelevant as we continue to build Moodys Tax;

My Mom—always my cheerleader and big fan. You sacrificed so much for the success of your kids - obviously including me - and you're simply the best. Thanks Mom!;

Lynda Hunt—thanks for twenty-two years of running the show. You are an unbelievable person, dedicated to our organization and its success. Thanks for keeping me straight.; and

All of my friends—Riaz, Craig, Cameron to name a few—and my siblings—Debbie, Monica, Cory, Stephanie and Deny. Thanks for the support....it means a lot.

CHAPTER 1

Who Knows More About Taxes, Seinfeld or Kramer?

O ne of my favorite episodes of *Seinfeld* features a memorable exchange between Jerry and Kramer about tax write-offs. Kramer offers to help Jerry obtain a refund on his stereo, which is two years past the expiration of its warranty. A couple of days later, a package arrives for Jerry in the mail—which turns out to be his own smashed stereo. Kramer then bounces in and explains that he purposely broke the stereo because Jerry's warranty had expired, and therefore, the only way to get Jerry's money back is to cash in on the $400 insurance policy that Kramer had purchased from the post office.

"So you're going to make the post office pay for my new stereo?" Jerry asks incredulously.

"All these big companies, they write everything off," Kramer assures him.

As Jerry continues to poke holes in Kramer's scheme, Kramer keeps repeating the phrase "tax write-off" until Jerry finally calls his bluff, betting that Kramer doesn't even know what a write-off is. He happens to be right: Kramer has no idea how tax write-offs work, and neither does Jerry.

As I am someone who has devoted his career to understanding the nuances of taxes, including tax write-offs, this was one of my favorite television moments.

I have worked with countless individuals, both employees and business owners, and I understand that the inner workings of taxation and write-offs can seem arcane and mysterious to many people. And so I've made it my mission in life to translate these complexities into language that everyday people can understand.

Roughly 80 percent of people are employees at companies. For this group, it's relatively easy to pay taxes without really understanding them. But business owners enter a whole other world of possibilities, and investors navigate an even more intricate system. For many people in all of these groups, there is a great deal of confusion about even base-level issues.

What's taxed as income? Are there other base levels of tax, like excise taxes and property taxes, to consider? And how do they intersect with income taxes?

When it comes to income tax, people tend to breeze past the question of what base they're being taxed on. They don't consider what constitutes income, and regulations are widely divergent among different countries. (For instance, lottery winnings are taxable in the United States, but not in Canada.)

Misinformation Abounds

In my personal and professional experience, I have found that the level of knowledge about taxation in the general population is extremely weak. When I attend networking events, I always meet people who brag about how much money they make and what they do to save money on taxes. Ninety percent of the time, the actions they describe are flat-out wrong.

I remember one guy telling me, "I bought my lakefront cottage through my company because my buddy told me that would save me a lot in taxes."

"Well, you did, did you?" I replied. "And your buddy thinks that's a good move?"

Internally, I found myself debating whether to offer my expertise and burst his bubble by telling him that he'd just exposed himself to triple taxation, or let him continue to brag. I went with the latter because hanging out at cocktail parties and hearing about tax mythology is quite fun.

Fake charitable donations were a big scam in Canada for more than two decades. They're not as common anymore because the Canada Revenue Agency finally caught on and started reassessing people. Promoters told these poor victims that if they donated $1,000, they could get a $5,000—or more—charitable-donation receipt. After they emptied their pockets, they found out that their money went straight into the hands of the promoter, and the $5,000 receipt would, in effect, be worthless. I'll examine this topic further in subsequent chapters because it was a prominent issue for many.

I'm writing this book because I want readers to be better informed about their own situations, and I want them to examine the national policy implications of our tax system. The first half of the book is about understanding your taxes on a personal level. I've found that many sophisticated people look at tax planning as an annual chore that can be ignored for the rest of the year. This is the wrong way to think about it. It's a movie, not a snapshot—something that should be seen as ongoing. I know plenty of businesspeople who lack that awareness and pay sorely for it. I also hope to clear up some of the rampant misinformation out there.

The second half of the book will delve into my recommendations for reforming taxation in a way that benefits society on a grander scale. What are we entitled to? And how should we be taxed? Those are deep policy questions that most people are ill-equipped to comment on, but I believe my personal and professional background gives me a unique perspective on these matters.

Who Am I?

As a child growing up in Fort McMurray, Alberta, I watched my parents struggle to raise our family. My stepfather was a restless soul who was always looking for opportunities to do things differently. Although he could have taken the easy route and continued to work at the large oil sands plant where he was making good money, he decided to take a risk and open a go-kart track in our recreation-starved town. That risk turned out to be a gold mine. In the off-season, he continued to look for other opportunities, eventually opening a milk delivery business and a firewood delivery service.

My mom, who also had an entrepreneurial spirit, was always looking for ways for her kids to earn extra money. She helped us pick up bottles and sell Christmas cards door to door, and she assisted us with our paper route and other activities, all so that she could demonstrate that it was not easy to make a living.

By their example, my parents taught us some very valuable lessons:

- The status quo is not always the best way.
- Look for opportunities (they may be right under your nose).
- Challenge norms.
- Be creative in developing new paths.
- Don't be afraid to take informed and calculated risks, even if you're criticized for it.

These lessons have formed my leadership style, my values, and my perspective. I will never forget that I'm only one or two events away from being brought back to my humble beginnings, and I serve my clients with that in mind.

My unique talent is my ability to put complex material into plain English, which helps me to gain my clients' trust. I never want my meetings to be about sales. Instead, I want to convey trustworthiness because trust is paramount when you have to put your tax affairs in someone else's hands.

I believe you should be able to trust your tax advisor implicitly, and at the end of the day, I'm not concerned about whether a client comes on board or not; I just want to work with people who are capable of having a trusting relationship.

Who Is a Tax Expert?

I've always enjoyed the study and practice of tax. However, I'm convinced that the traditional way of practicing tax—either as part of a traditional accounting firm or as part of a general-practice law firm supporting other lawyers—is not the way to do it. I have always felt that tax is one of those rare practice areas that demand that two different kinds of professionals—in this case, accountants and lawyers—embrace working together, rather than apart.

I enjoy challenging the traditional view that these professions are not businesses. For far too long, my peers have not embraced fundamental principles of business such as client service, marketing, and identifying new opportunities for their clients; instead, they fall back on their view that these professions are above being treated as businesses.

One thing that many people aren't aware of is that in Canada, anybody can claim to be an accountant and put out a shingle to start doing business.

There's no regulation governing the use of titles like "accountant" or "specialist" by untrained professionals.

Nobody can claim to be a lawyer without attending law school or passing the necessary exams, but if my sister wanted to open up Debbie's Tax Specialist accounting firm, she could legally do it tomorrow, even though she has no expertise in the area.

I believe that if you go through the rigor of training and then spend your career meeting the continuing obligations that are set out by a governing body, then you're part of an exclusive club. One of the benefits of that club is that there's a monopoly on providing that service: There's a monopoly on legal services. There's a monopoly on medical services. And there are good reasons for protecting those monopolies—it's in the interest of protecting the public. And yet, for some reason, that public interest concern doesn't seem to be operational when it comes to accounting or tax, which is a frustrating disconnect.

In Canada, there are accountants, like me, who do taxes, and there are tax lawyers. But most of these lawyers have no LLM, because there are very few schools in Canada that offer LLMs. Roughly 1 percent of lawyers practice tax, but the number of accountants who practice tax, or give tax advice—or *think* they can give tax advice—is much larger.

There are approximately 220,000 accountants in Canada, and virtually all of them who are in public practice use tax services as a way to attract work. Many call themselves tax experts or specialists. I can't point to an exact statistic, but I've found that fewer than 1 percent of accountants are true tax experts or specialists, and the public has no way of identifying that 1 percent because there is no regulation of these claims. Law societies are generally strict about a lawyer calling himself a tax expert or a specialist, but the accounting profession is not.

Because of this, I've spent years advocating for legislation governing who can call himself a tax expert in Canada. The UK has what's called a Chartered Tax Advisor designation, which is a separate designation from "lawyer" or "chartered accountant." Obtaining this designation requires a very rigorous education, and the upshot of this is that the British public has a better way to identify where to go for tax advice, and it recognizes the difference between hiring a chartered tax advisor and seeking out a "plain vanilla" lawyer or accountant. We need that in North America in order to protect the public interest, and I will continue to fight for it.

The Role of Confidentiality

One reason people turn to lawyers rather than accountants to handle their taxes is that lawyers have *privileged* communications, which are significantly different from *confidential* communications.

Early in my career, I had a problem with lawyers who tried to take work away from me by telling prospective clients that accountants could be forced to turn people in to the Canada Revenue Agency, whereas they, as lawyers, couldn't because of the rules governing client-privileged communications. There were full-sized billboards and television advertisements that aggressively asked, "Did you know that your accountants can turn you in? Only our lawyers can protect your interests and not be forced to turn you in."

In reality, accountants rarely have to turn over their communications with their clients. I found it distasteful that these lawyers were resorting to presenting accountants as bogeymen. I saw it as a cheap way for them to differentiate themselves from accountants, and possibly to attract people who had something to hide, or who were just secretive and mistrustful of government by nature.

My frustration with these advertisements and their implications led me to study up on privileged communications.

Based on my naïve and uneducated first impressions, I initially believed that accountants should have privileged-like communications when dealing with tax matters. As I studied the issue further, I began to understand the historical origins and policy intent of privileged communications.

Now I understand that there's no way that accountants should have privileged communications with their clients; that's an access-to-justice issue. However, there are still lawyers who don't completely understand the meaning of privileged communications and thus are quick to use this concept as a distasteful weapon in their marketing.

I think accountants should have statutory confidentiality— which is very different from privilege—when dealing with certain types of tax or planning matters that could eventually get into litigation, but *not* privileged communications when dealing with criminal matters. This could level the playing field between lawyers and accountants and make it easier for clients to pick the right tax advisor.

Statutory confidentiality for accountants would enable taxpayers to seek the best tax advice/advisor, as opposed to going to a lawyer simply for the benefit of privileged communications. Without some form of statutory confidentiality, tax lawyers have a leg up on accountants . . . to the detriment of clients who might be better served by accountants than lawyers. But for many, the allure of privilege outweighs the desire for the best advice or service.

This is one of the reasons why our practice operates as a law firm *and* as an accounting firm. I lead both the law firm and accounting firm, but when acting through the law firm, I obviously involve lawyers with all our client accounts in order to ensure privileged communications. If accountants had something that came close to the protections that lawyers have, we could develop a much more efficient system.

It's Time for Real Reform

My firm, Moodys Tax Law LLP, aspires to be the premier cross-border tax law/advisory firm in Canada, and is considered a thought leader in such matters. Our team is sought after for client advice and policy views by tax administrators, tax policy makers, government officials, academics, and tax professionals.

I have taken on virtually every single prominent role in the tax profession in Canada, and now I'm looking to find out what else I can do. I've used my leadership positions to understand how things work and where we can make positive changes, and to forge relationships with politicians to let them know that we need to work together to improve the system.

On balance, I think our society works pretty well. That being said, the last time Canada had comprehensive tax review and reform was in 1962, when we had a Royal Commission on Taxation, which took four years to release its report in 1966. It then took another six years to debate the report before a good chunk of the recommendations could finally be implemented.

Whatever happened to just taking the political hats off for a minute and looking at what's good for society? This seems unrealistic in this day and age, but from 1962 to 1966, Canadians *did* take off their political hats, and they came together. An independent commission was appointed to advise the government on what Canada's tax policies should be. I think that's necessary again now, rather than having politicians foist ideas upon us. I'm ready for reform, but let's do it the right way.

Throughout this book, I will help you become more informed about the complexities of the tax system by translating ideas that can help you save money and avoid making mistakes into language that's easy to understand. I will also share more of my thoughts on improving the overall system. Welcome aboard!

CHAPTER 2

You're Probably Paying More Taxes Than You Should Be

Tax planning is about more than simply looking at your current tax bill. It's about planning for what your future tax bill will be, and ultimately, it's about knowing which errors might cost you. Scotiabank has a brilliant marketing slogan that I wish I'd come up with myself: "*You're richer than you think.*" I've found that most of my clients are richer than they think when tax opportunities are taken into account.

Often, people focus too much on whether they can claim a current deduction or how much their immediate tax liability/refund will be. My goal is to get them to think through to their endgame and figure out what they're actually trying to do. I've found that if clients invest some time in learning about their overall tax situation, they will probably find opportunities to save that they didn't know existed. From that perspective, most people are richer than they think they are. In fact, I've found that roughly eight out of ten clients can do better than they think they can in terms of saving on tax.

For an employee, there are very limited opportunities, but those opportunities should be considered. For a businessperson, there is much more to consider when structuring their affairs to either defer tax or save tax, but it starts with understanding their individual life objectives. What are their "dangers, opportunities, and strengths" so a fulsome plan can be developed that doesn't let the "tax tail wag the dog?"

Many people who come to our practice don't know how to plan to protect their resources after death. They don't know how to properly leave money to their kids without losing a good chunk of it to taxes, and they don't understand how their philanthropic objectives fit with their overall estate plan. Some are unaware of how acquiring a life insurance policy might magnify their wealth while providing a runway for tax savings. I don't get paid for selling insurance, but it makes sense for me to mention that option when discussing estate planning. Just by having a short conversation, my clients can end up richer than they thought they were, and so can their descendants. And that's my objective.

We Give You Our A-Team

If you're an individual with private corporations and/or trusts, the major accounting and law firms might not be the best people to handle your affairs in a way that considers your particular needs and goals. There are a number of reasons why this is the case, but perhaps the biggest one is that their A-team is rarely assigned to handle private client affairs. Errors or omissions can occur because these advisors often do not have time to pay

MAKING LIFE LESS TAXING

full attention to the difficulty of complex situations. In many cases, the firms are part of an assembly line, and they just want your business off their desks as soon as possible so that they can move on to the next file.

The A-teams at these major firms in Canada are often busy working on the business of major corporations, where it is likely that the majority of profits are made through their largest files, rather than through their dealings with private clients. They continue to serve private clients because it can be profitable— but, again, it's often done with an assembly-line approach. That approach will generally not afford the advisors time to truly understand their clients—to learn what makes them tick and what their dangers, opportunities, and strengths are—to ensure that the best overall advice is given.

On many occasions, our team has found mistakes in the files of clients who worked with firms before coming to us. Of course, we're not infallible either; we make mistakes too. But not as many. We try very hard to provide A-team services for clients in the private-client space, and we want to serve people who aren't being well served. It's unfair to pay Ritz-Carlton prices only to discover you're staying at the Motel 6.

Some of our top clients pay significant amounts of money to our firm. When I talk to these clients, who can afford to pay whomever they want, I ask them why they've chosen to work with us. Many have expressed that it's because they're completely ignored by other firms. For example, they might turn to one of the brand-name firms for help with an audit because their bank requires them to have an audit and a brand-name firm is certainly well recognized by a bank. But ultimately,

15

many of those clients use those firms as an insurance policy and are buying a commodity rather than getting value-added services like tax assistance. They want to be able to pluck out the best talent and know they're entering into a trusting relationship, which is what they get from us.

Assessing the Big Picture

Another reason firms/advisors can make mistakes is that many do not take a top-down approach that examines the client's bigger picture. For instance, are the advisors looking at everything the client owns and how such assets fit into their overall objectives? A client might own a company, interests in a partnership, beneficial interests in a trust, and property in the United States and Europe. Unless someone is taking the time to thoroughly understand the overall picture and how it fits within the client's tax, reporting, and business objectives, then such planning is likely suboptimal.

I've found that in Canada, the family offices of a certain size do a pretty good job of considering all these elements. But many others aren't given the time or the resources to pull these disparate pieces together.

Firms like ours attempt to take a family-office approach and apply our expertise on the tax side. If it's obvious that a client needs advice in other areas, we'll bring in outside experts. That doesn't mean we're going to need to outsource everything, but we're going to get them the advice that they need.

I've found that some larger firms are impersonal. At such firms, they don't care who you are or what ultimately makes you tick. Public companies can be very similar. They often don't think beyond their latest quarterly profits or whether they've met budget expectations or analyst expectations. They're short-term thinkers focused on short-term profits.

That model doesn't work very well with private clients because, for them, it's about their own lives. It's about what they're trying to achieve with their money: philanthropic goals, their kids' goals, their own goals. What do they do with their money once they're successful? Do they keep building? If so, why? How does that fit in with their plan? Many larger firms are just not structured to think about these concerns.

One of the first things I do with new or prospective clients is ask them specific questions about how they see their future. If they can answer these questions clearly, I know that we can adjust our planning to fit their objectives. Once I figure out what their objectives are, we dig into the facts.

I'll ask the client how she is operating her business right now. If it's through a corporation, I'll delve into the pros and cons of that decision. Choosing an entity is one of the most important decisions a business owner has to make. There are several forms to choose from, each of which generates different legal and tax consequences, and there isn't one form of entity that's right for every type of business owner. Moreover, this decision can have a major impact on taxes.

Entity selection is something in which to invest a great deal of time in order to maximize savings or deferral. The first question I ask is where the person is trying to do business. Are they trying to do business in Canada, the United States, or both? Or in other parts of the world? In our practice, it's generally Canada, although a large percentage does business in the United States as well. Many people are not sure if they should be carrying out their US-based business through a Canadian corporation. US tax reform has turned entity selection completely upside down in terms of cross-border planning.

As part of the entity selection, we look at who should hold those entities' interests. Should it be the individual? Should it be a trust? Should it be a corporation, like a holding company? And there's no shortage of pros and cons—for both tax and non-tax reasons—to consider when making those choices.

We also begin poking into questions about the future. What are they planning to do in the future? What are their revenues? What profits are they expecting? What are the liability/risk concerns? Are they planning to do work anywhere else? What's their overall wealth objective? How much do they want to make before they retire? Do they have a will? If they die unexpectedly, where's their wealth going?

I typically dive into those topics and then look at historical returns, both corporate and personal, to determine if there are any errors. Close to half the time, there *are* errors, or things could certainly be structured better or more targeted.

These might even be high-/ultra-high-net-worth people who may have operations in the United States and Canada. Any movement of income between the two countries will typically involve the use of foreign tax credits to make sure there's no double taxation. People who pay tax in the US had better make sure to use that as a foreign tax credit in Canada to avoid double taxation. That's a pretty difficult area of tax law, and I would say that seven times out of ten, there are screw-ups in such dealings.

We often find that many people are not getting what they need in terms of estate planning. They may be getting immediate good advice on whether an expenditure is deductible, for example, but it's often shortsighted. The advisor may have offered good advice given the current conditions, but what happens if this client gets divorced or becomes disabled? Has anybody thought about this?

Since I've known many of my clients for decades, I've been with them through storms in their personal lives. When a client mentions marital problems, I look to ensure that we've built plans that consider his/her interests if the marriage dissolves. I'm not going to say that I can create a foolproof structure, but we consider that contingency in the planning phase.

Many plans fail to consider the what-ifs: death, divorce, disability, and bankruptcy should be baked into all your plans. What kind of ramifications do these possibilities have, not just for the individual's taxes, but also for the company's? If there's going to be a split, does that mean the company is going to have to be sold to satisfy divorce obligations? If so, would selling the business be akin to taking the golden goose and chopping off its head? If so, a better scenario for both parties must be considered.

Smart choices result from asking what-ifs and engaging in proactive thinking. Many people are hopers, dreamers, and wishers; they're not very goal-driven. But if you apply a goal-driven mentality to your work and ask the what-ifs, it's amazing what you'll find.

When I'm building my team by interviewing candidates, I ask them similar questions to those that I ask clients. If I get an answer that speaks in terms of hoping and wishing, I give him or her one more chance and say, "I'm not looking for your hopes or wishes; I'm looking for what your measurable goals are." If he or she can figure out how to redirect his or her sentiments into proper answers, I will consider his or her application. But if he or she can't, I dismiss him or her immediately. I don't care how smart he or she is, or whether I think he or she could add to my practice; I will not hire that person.

I want to work with people who think proactively and consider the client's goals. And from a selfish perspective, I don't want to work with a dreamer and a drifter; I want somebody who can help achieve the firm's goals and my own. Without a clear sense of one's own goals, it's impossible to steer clients in the right direction.

Canadian and American Are Different Languages

At my firm, we like to say that Canadians don't speak American very well, and Americans don't speak Canadian very well. The typical model at larger firms is that Canadians work on the Canadian matters only and ship the US matters to their US colleagues. In many cases, they literally ship papers to the United States, and their colleagues across the border have to figure out what to do and send them back. But there's no reconciliation, because the Canadians don't speak American, and the Americans don't speak Canadian.

So we've developed our firm internally, and by design, so that both the Americans and the Canadians are working in-house. We don't train Canadians to be US tax advisors/preparers because we don't think that works, and vice versa. The advantage is that they can speak to each other in person. We can enlist people from both countries to make sure that the plan and the implementation sync up and work together, which yields powerful results.

Most firms allow the Canadians to speak Canadian and the Americans to speak American, which makes their overall coordination weak. Sometimes the Canadians are trained to speak American, which doesn't work well either. Taxes in the US are completely different from Canadian taxes, and you can't just have a Canadian-trained person take a few courses and consider him a US expert. All of our US people are born, raised, educated, and trained in the United States.

If you are a Canadian businessperson who operates in the United States, it's essential to make sure that you're not being exposed to long-term double taxation and that all of your reporting obligations are being met. It is extremely important to coordinate carefully with the American tax people and the Canadian tax people to see that the plan works conceptually. This coordination routinely falls to the wayside with Canadian advisors and US advisors who aren't working in concert. Coordinating cash movements from a US entity to Canada is very important to avoid double taxation. We see mismatches all the time. Not good.

Other issues can arise from a Canadian expanding his or her business into the United States, and these must be co-ordinated carefully. An American expanding business into Canada will face the same issues, but now in reverse. A US citizen, particularly someone with the stature of a CEO, who is imported from the United States, must be handled carefully. Professional athletes who are US citizens and play in Canada need to learn to maximize their after-tax amounts on their bonuses and salaries.

Other issues can occur after death. When a Canada-residing US citizen with a high net worth dies, he or she is subject to the US estate tax law. Coordinating that with Canada's deemed disposition on death regime is not easy, and it can lead to a significant depletion of wealth. That's something that many people don't think through.

The United States loves its reporting regimes, especially for US citizens who live in other countries. These expatriates have to provide numerous reports, which can cause angst and exposure to significant penalties if they miss a report. Many Canadian and US practitioners simply don't have sufficient knowledge about this.

The issues I'm describing are multimillion-dollar liabilities that would fall through the cracks at some firms because no one would ever notice. People can go through their entire careers and never know that they left tens of millions of dollars in tax savings on the table because no one was aware of these issues.

These are all reasons why we run our firm with a strong focus on the clients' goals and an eye on the what-ifs, and this is why we use native experts to handle these complex matters.

CHAPTER 3

Every Day Should Be Tax Day, Not Just April 30

Got plans for tonight?

Here's an idea: How about sitting down and doing your taxes?

No, I'm not kidding; I'm dead serious. Doing your taxes tonight makes perfect sense.

The odds are very good—364 to one, to be exact—that today, the day you're reading this, isn't April 30, the deadline for filing tax returns in Canada (and not, coincidentally, the day when far too many Canadians decide it's finally time to figure out exactly how much they owe the government). This is why reviewing your tax obligation tonight makes perfect sense. There is no "right" day to think about it—unless you don't mind paying more than you have to or taking the risk of paying less than you owe. If you want to minimize what you'll owe on April 30, then every day—all 365 of them—is the "right" day to think about your taxes.

Most Canadians don't pay much attention to their taxes until around the first day of November, when the media starts publishing stories about what you should do before the end of the year.

Once they've gotten those stories out of the way, they go dark again until sometime in February, when they start publishing advice for you to consider ahead of the April 30 filing deadline.

Those stories show up every year like clockwork—but they're not for you. They lack depth. They're geared toward the average Joe who doesn't really want to think about taxes.

That's not you. You need to be thinking on a much broader scale.

You need to think about taxes as if they were exercise. You can't sit on the couch, getting fat on cheese puffs and beer all year, and then look in the mirror on the day after Christmas, hop onto an elliptical machine, put the pedal to the metal, and be in great shape by New Year's Eve.

It would be great if we could actually do that, but we know better. Exercise and nutrition are lifelong pursuits—and so is tax planning.

Successful business owners and wealthy individuals who want to leave every dollar they can to their successors, heirs, and/or charity can't allow themselves to fall into the media-created trap of thinking about their taxes only once a year. They need to think about them every day, and they need to plan their affairs accordingly, because they—*you*—are not the average Joe those newspaper and magazine stories are written for.

You're very different from a salaried worker who puts in forty hours a week and gets a paycheck every Friday. You can't dump a big box filled with statements and receipts on your accountant's desk on the last week of April every year and hope for the best— because the best may have already slipped through your fingers, and now it's too late to get it back.

What do you think you'll do when your accountant looks up from behind that huge mountain of paper you've dropped in front of him and says it's too late to do some of the things you could have done to minimize your payments?

What are you going to do if you bought some expensive equipment last year, and now he's telling you that you would have done better from a tax perspective if you'd leased it?

What if you had some legal expenses, and you paid your lawyer without asking your accountant if those expenses were deductible?

If you reflexively buy something—if you just write a check every time you get a bill—you may be ignoring an alternative that can lower your tax payments. And if you don't even consider your options, if you just dump everything in your accountant's lap every April and tell him to do your taxes . . .

What do you think you'll say when your accountant asks why you didn't get him on the phone immediately, when he could have told you to do things differently?

I know what you'll say: nothing—because there'll be nothing *to* say. It'll be too late. You blew it.

You need to keep these things in mind at all times, not just in late April. And if you're not the sort of person who can do that, then maybe you need to find a tax expert who can—someone who will be proactively involved in your financial affairs and will keep all those things in mind for you.

Retaining someone to do that comes with a price, of course. But what you pay may be far less than what he'll save for you. A proactive tax consultant can make a big impact on your bottom line.

———————————

When we meet with clients for the first time, we start out by discussing their "lifetime extender"—what they want their life and business to become—and their "DOS[1]": Dangers, Opportunities, and Strengths, as discussed earlier. Ultimately, we're interested in our clients' goals. We want to help them achieve their goals.

We then determine whether their business is financially and legally structured properly.

Then I ask what they expect to do with their wealth—how they want it to fuel their retirement and where they want their assets to go when they die.

Do they intend to sell their business someday? Do they plan to pass it on to their heirs or someone they're close to? If there's nobody they want to leave it to, do they want to give what's left to charity?

This is a high-level approach, but it's essential because I believe in doing things right, and I want my clients to feel the same way.

We make sure that all the necessary legal documents—wills, powers of attorney, advanced directives, etc.—are in place, and then we get down to the details:

---

[1] DOS is a concept developed and explained through their coaching programs. More at https://www.strategiccoach.com

How do we structure for maximum tax deferral or tax savings?

Do we need to tweak your legal structure to achieve your objectives?

Should we look at limited partnerships? Corporations? Trusts?

Do you plan on leaving Canada someday? If you do, then we need to plan for that today because you'll likely want to hold your assets differently.

And finally, we discuss that thing we hate to think about, but know we must: Have you planned for what will happen if you die unexpectedly? It's an uncomfortable topic, but it can happen—and we want to make sure you'll have everything in place if it happens to you.

———•———

Those are just the macro issues we discuss with our clients and keep in mind for them throughout the year so they don't have to.

Once those issues are settled, we drill down into the micro ones, the day-to-day minutiae.

Let's say your company is putting up a new building. Do you know the best way to do that from a tax perspective?

Maybe, both for tax advantages and for risk protection, you should create a new legal entity to own that building.

Or, on the other hand, maybe you shouldn't.

Are you qualified to balance the pros and cons and reach the right decision? Do you know the details of risk insurance and tax issues well enough to do what's best for your business?

If you're not absolutely sure that you are qualified, then you need help, because this is the sort of thing you can't afford to get wrong.

You might want to put your new building into a limited partnership, or a new corporation, or a trust—some sort of entity that is separate from your operating business. If you do that, you might reduce your risk of losing the building if something awful happens to your business.

Setting up a new entity to own your building would likely add to your administrative costs, and it probably wouldn't help much to reduce your tax liability—but it might help you protect and maximize your assets.

Or maybe it wouldn't.

And maybe—no, make that *probably*—you don't actually know for sure, which is why you should consult with a lawyer and a tax consultant before you make a major decision of this sort.

You need to keep this in mind at all times so you can make well-informed decisions as your business grows. Always ask yourself the following questions: Can I do this myself, or can I use some help? Are the fees that would be associated with good advice a "cost" or an "investment"?

───── • ─────

One of the most commonly used structures in Canada is the holding company. You'll meet with your accountant, and she'll say, "Let's set up a holding company that you'll own, and then the holding company will own all of the shares of your operating company."

If you do that, you'll operate your business out of your wholly owned subsidiary, and you'll put your valuable assets, like cash and real estate, into the holding company.

If your operating company makes a lot of money, it will pay a dividend to your holding company—and in many cases, that dividend will be tax-deferred. This is a very effective way to strip assets out of your operating company.

But there's a hitch:

If you die, or if you sell, you're likely limiting yourself to an asset sale. If you want to sell your operating business, either your holding company will have to sell its shares, or you'll have to sell your shares of the holding company. But nobody's going to buy the shares of the holding company, because it would mean you're selling the underlying cash and real estate inside it. And that would add to the purchase price. So going this route can be very limiting.

Now consider an alternative:

If you own your business through a corporation, and the shares of such are qualified small-business corporation shares, you can take advantage of Canada's capital gains exemption if you sell your shares of your operating company personally.

If you do that, you can get roughly the first $850,000 of your gain tax-free.

That's a pretty lucrative deduction—but you get it only if you sell your shares personally. If you set up a holding company to own shares of your operating company, you can't get that $850,000 without paying taxes on it.

These are just some of the myriad options that you need to consider as you structure your business to maximize the amount of your money you can keep in your hands—and out of the government's.

There's one more thing you want to be thinking about as you seek maximum profit: You built all of this. You're in charge of it all. Now how do you get paid?

Here's one option: You'll create a private corporation to carry on your business so you can benefit from the low corporate tax rate, which is about 10–12 percent on roughly the first $500,000 of business profits that are earned from Canadian activities. And as long as you don't have a lifestyle that burns away all your profits, you can build significant assets using that low tax rate.

But what if you need more? How can you get more than 10 percent?

There are lots of ways.

You can put your family members on the payroll and pay them reasonable salaries for legitimate efforts expended. You can give them shares in the company so they can collect dividends, subject to the below discussion. You can create a trust to which the company pays dividends and make your family members the beneficiaries of the trust who receive dividends, again, subject to the below.

We're talking about income splitting—remunerating family members to the extent that is legally allowed. For decades, it's been an important planning tool in Canada, a great way to cover everyone's lifestyle and living expenses.

But it isn't easy. In 2018, the government revised the Tax on Split Income (TOSI) law, adding a series of very complex rules that made it harder to pay family members.

If, for example, your teenager is a direct or indirect share-holder in your business, and she gets paid a dividend each year, the government can look at whether she actually "earned" her dividend. And if it rules that she didn't, she'll wind up paying the highest marginal tax rate on her dividend.

So income splitting is still a great way to minimize your taxes, but it isn't as easy as it used to be. You need to know the law, and that's harder than ever now. The rules are so complicated that even the average accountant can't understand them.

When the average business owner can't make sense of the rules, and his accountant can't either, you're going to have a lot of noncompliance, both inadvertent and intentional. And then a lot of people will get caught, and they'll end up paying either a lot more in taxes or a lot more to fight an assessment—all because they didn't understand what they had to do in the first place.

When innocent, well-intentioned business owners can't comply with the law because they can't make heads or tails of it, that's a societal problem. Whether they own a tiny business or even a good-sized one, they shouldn't have to consult with an expensive tax expert to decipher a law that is supposed to apply across the board. That reflects a systemic breakdown. It's wrong.

———————

There's another thing you should keep in mind every day of the year, and not just when April rolls around: it's what I call your revenue recognition policy.

In Canada, your business income—with very few exceptions—is taxed on an accrued basis. If you issued an invoice for services rendered in November 2018, but you didn't get paid until February 2019, the amount you charged is considered taxable income for 2018.

You pay taxes on the year you do the work, not the year you get paid for it. If you never get paid, you can take a deduction—but that might not happen for a couple of years.

This is another reason you may need a tax specialist who will be looking out for you every day of the year.

There are ways to match your tax payments with your cash receipts, and there are tools to help you make sure you don't lose sight of any unpaid invoices from work you've completed or from projects still in progress.

But can you stay on top of all of this?

If you have an expert who knows all the minuscule details of the tax laws, you can reduce your exposure in cases like this.

I have never met anyone who woke up in the morning, opened the window shades, stretched his arms out wide, and said to himself, "I'm really psyched. I can't wait to pay some taxes today!"

Nobody likes paying taxes. We know they provide services that all of us take advantage of every day, but we still hate paying them. We want to pay as little as the law allows, and we want to latch on to every possible opportunity to minimize. But that's hard to do because the laws can be very hard to decipher.

Consider legal fees, for example. Sometimes they can be deducted, sometimes they can't. Do you know when they can?

Consider franchise fees. If you pay a consultant to help you look for and buy a franchise, is that a deductible cost? According to the law, the original cost of acquiring the franchise is considered an asset, which is amortizable over time. But ongoing fees like royalties are likely deductible.

Consider your tax liability if you get sued and settle out of court. Is what you pay deductible? Sometimes it is; sometimes it isn't.

So do you deduct or not? And whichever you choose, will you be right?

You'd better be—because whether you overpay or underpay, you risk paying a lot if you're wrong.

I remember the case of a company that received $2 million in upfront deposits. The company had reported the deposits in its accounting records as a liability since it had not yet performed any services and the deposits were refundable. That company came to us when it discovered that, according to Canadian tax law, the $2 million deposit it collected at the start of its project was taxable upon receipt. There were some very specific rules that would have helped the company defer the income until it actually did the work, but they didn't apply in this case.

We ultimately found a solution to keep the owner on the straight and narrow. We assisted the client in negotiating a change in the wording of the contract to make some of the upfront deposit fit within the narrow exceptions that were allowed.

But we couldn't fix everything—and what we couldn't fix had to come out of the client's pocket. He didn't have to pay the full amount he owed on the $2 million, but he had to pay more than he would have if he'd come to us in the first place.

It was painful, and he came to us too late to avert that pain.

⎯⎯⎯◆⎯⎯⎯

That's what can happen when a taxpayer unknowingly pays less than he owes. But the opposite situation—a taxpayer paying too much because an advisor thinks something isn't deductible when it actually is—is just as bad.

Let's say you're the owner of a building, and you're leasing space to a tenant, and your arrangement calls for you to spend a hundred grand on making leasehold improvements to the tenant's satisfaction.

The typical advisor will capitalize those leasehold improvements on your books to make them deductible over time.

But in some cases, you're allowed to deduct that $100,000 immediately—because you, the landlord, are expected to incur reasonable recurring expenses on an ongoing basis. If your advisor doesn't know that (because he hasn't kept up with the case law or CRA administrative practice), well, that's just too bad.

Advisors miss stuff like this all the time. But when they do, *you* are the one who doesn't get to keep the money that's rightfully yours.

If you pay too little, you risk getting caught. And if you get caught, you'll have to pay what you owe *plus* possible penalties and interest.

So you don't want to pay too little.

But you don't want to pay too much either, because if you do, the government isn't going to take the high road, look for all the opportunities you didn't notice, and send you a check for the difference. It'll just keep what you paid. It won't even say thank you.

CHAPTER 4

Tax Avoidance versus Tax Evasion: Are You Playing Audit Roulette?

The saying goes, "If at first you don't succeed, try, try again." But there are some things we shouldn't try in the first place, no matter how well we think we might do if we give them a shot.

Take heart surgery, for example. My dentist has great hands, and I think he'd be a very good heart surgeon. But if I ever need bypass surgery, I assure you, I'm not going to let him scrub up and grab a scalpel. I don't have to tell you why; the reason is obvious. But it's not so obvious in the tax world.

Some accountants will tell you that they're well versed in the tax laws, and that they make sure their clients pay only what they must—not a penny more. And the average person will believe them, because he's been told that accountants know everything there is to know about taxes. But that's a myth.

The typical accountant has very minimal tax training and very minimal skills in applying tax laws. If he didn't have software to help him, he would struggle mightily.

That's because his core training is in accounting. I have no doubt that he's a whiz with an income statement and a balance sheet, and that he's been trained on basic tax concepts and foundations, and on how the law basically works—but that's it. If he isn't diving into the Income Tax Act every day, I don't care how good an accountant he is. His understanding of tax law will be basic at best, and weak at worst.

Think of this in terms of health care. The average accountant is a general practitioner, not a specialist. Just as you'd go see your family doctor for a persistent cough or a bad cold, you'd sit down with an average accountant to help you complete an average tax return.

But if you're a business owner who is legally entitled to deduct numerous expenses and who routinely files a complicated tax return, you need more than a general practitioner. You need a specialist, because Canada's tax laws have become very complex over the years—and the average accountant just can't keep up.

For the average consumer of accounting services, this isn't an issue because it doesn't really affect him much. He gets a paycheck, and he either submits a simple tax return, or, if he doesn't feel comfortable preparing it himself, he pays an accountant to do it for him. But a business owner is not a salaried employee. If your income derives from more than a regular paycheck, you need a specialist, someone who has an intimate knowledge and understanding of the tax law—someone who will keep you from playing a game I call audit roulette.

I've encountered far too many people in business who think they're entitled to claim just about every penny they spend as tax-deductible business expenses. Second homes, vacations, artwork, jewelry, cars, dinners at fancy restaurants—they think all they have to do is say they were business expenses, and the government will be too stupid to ask questions.

They think, *Let them come after me. I'm really smart. The tax department is too dumb to outwit a brilliant thinker like me.* That's audit roulette. It's claiming deductions or taking positions you know you're not entitled to—or you suspect they might be legitimate, but you're not really sure—and hoping the government doesn't flag your tax return for an audit. And the truth is, there's a decent chance that it won't. Your odds are good because roughly 3 percent of taxpayers get audited.

But look at it this way: If you're in a room with thirty-two friends and you know one of you is going to get audited, do you feel comfortable that it won't be you? If you deducted expenses that you weren't entitled to, are you willing to risk paying a substantial penalty and compounding interest—in addition to what you should have paid in the first place—if the government decides to scrutinize your return? Or, if you've knowingly gone too far, are you willing to risk being charged with a crime? That's what you're doing when you push the envelope.

Whether you run a corporation or you're a sole proprietor, you can't just decide that all your expenses are business-related. If you take your wife with you on a business trip, and you spend a little time talking business, that doesn't entitle you to deduct her entire trip. If you buy a summer cottage and you bring in a desk with a laptop and a printer, that doesn't make it a company office building.

Maybe you think it does—but there's a good chance the government won't. And there's an even better chance that the government will win the argument, and you'll find yourself forced to pay a very significant penalty.

You'll end up saying, "I bought a cottage through my company. That's so dumb. I can't believe I did that." And that's when you'll wish you'd had a tax expert working with you before you submitted your return.

———•———

If you buy a personal asset through a corporation, the Canada Revenue Agency will most likely consider that purchase to be a shareholder benefit—meaning that the company made the purchase, and you benefited from it. Once it's made that decision, the government will want to determine the quantum of the benefit—just how much value it had for you.

This happens because you bypassed the normal way to buy personal assets: taking money out of your corporation, paying personal taxes on what you took out, and then using your after-tax money to buy whatever you wanted—a cottage, a car, a swimming pool, whatever. By having your company buy the asset, you avoided paying personal taxes, so the government will want to tax you on the quantum of benefit you received. It will deem such computed amount to be an income inclusion.

Let's say your company bought a summer cottage, and you spent ten nights in it. Some people think the quantum of benefit is comparable to what you would pay to stay in a hotel room.

If you would pay $500 a night, that's a $5,000 taxable benefit out of the corporation—and therefore, you would pay personal tax on $5,000.

But that isn't how it works. In a case like this, the courts would say, "Okay, what was the cost of that property? Oh, you paid $500,000 to buy it? What would the rate of return have been if the company didn't invest in a personal-use property?"

That appropriate rate of return will be deemed your income inclusion—even though you received no money. And that can lead to double taxation, or even triple taxation, because you decided to hold personal-use assets in a corporation.

That's really dumb, and it's very common—because people who don't understand the tax laws often think this can be an effective plan. And it'll work—right up until your number comes up in the audit roulette wheel.

It's unlikely that you'll go to prison for doing something like that. If you did it on your own, you probably didn't know any better. If you relied upon the advice of your accountant, advisor, or friend, chances are, he didn't know any better either. So what you did wasn't criminal—no wrongdoing was intended. But it sure was silly. You wandered into an area that you thought you knew, but you didn't. And now your ignorance is going to cost you.

Business owners do all sorts of silly things when they don't know the tax laws. One area where they often get caught is putting their family members on payroll to take advantage of income splitting—but those family members don't do any work.

Let's say your kid is in college; he has no life experience and hardly any work experience. You decide that income splitting allows you to pay him a $50,000-a-year salary to stay in school. But would you do the same for someone who isn't a relative? I don't think you would—and neither will the government.

The government allows every individual to claim a basic exemption amount of roughly $12,000. That amount goes up every year, so let's place it at, say, $12,646. Because you own a business, your advisor may advise you to pay your college-aged kid exactly that amount—even if he does nothing to earn it—because he has no other income, and that's how much he can claim as his personal exemption.

So your company pays your kid $12,646 and claims a deduction of that amount. Your son owes no income tax, and everyone's happy—unless your number comes up at the audit roulette table. If that happens, the Income Tax Act won't let the business deduct the salary because your kid did no work. But at least he won't have to pay any personal tax because the amount was equal to his basic exemption.

But if you paid him $50,000, that's double trouble. The government won't let your business deduct the entire unreasonable payment (assuming that the entire $50,000 is unreasonable), *and* your kid will have to pay taxes on the $37,354 above his basic exemption. Now you're in double-taxation territory because you didn't know any better. Your company is paying more corporate tax, your kid is paying income tax, and you're feeling really silly.

People do stuff like this all the time because they don't know any better. They'll take their spouse out to a fancy restaurant, enjoy some caviar and champagne while they wait for the Kobe steaks to arrive, and then call it a business meal and put it on the company's tab. And the babysitter who's watching the kids? They'll have the company pay for that too.

In fact, I've seen people pay their nannies and say it's a business expense because they wouldn't be able to work if they didn't have someone to watch the children. I've also seen people use their company credit cards to pay for their groceries, claiming they bought their milk, eggs, and peanut butter for business meals and entertainment.

Some people use company money to buy cars because why should they settle for a Chevy when the company can buy a Lamborghini and call it an investment? Once, I saw a family spend tens of thousands of dollars of their company's money on a "business trip"—a luxury Caribbean cruise.

That's well and good until someone discovers that the diamond ring you called a company investment is wrapped around your wife's finger, or until that Rembrandt you bought with company money is found hanging in the foyer of your home. If that happens, I promise you, the government will not agree that these were legitimate business expenses or "investments."

You just might get away with all of this though—because, as we mentioned earlier, you have roughly a 3 percent chance of getting audited. That chance is increasing as the algorithms for flagging questionable returns become more sophisticated—something worth thinking about when you're filing an aggressive return—but the odds might still be in your favor that you won't be audited.

Even if you do get audited, it's very unlikely that you'll end up behind bars. The government would have to charge you with criminal tax evasion and win a conviction. That rarely happens—unless your greed is just too outrageous to be ignored.

If you're merely stupid—if you bought your cottage through your business because your buddy did it and you thought it was okay—you'll just have to fork over a big pile of money if you get caught. But if you're knowingly buying groceries and liquor and cars and jewelry, and you're going on expensive vacations, and you're deducting all of these as business expenses, the more it looks like tax evasion. And that's a crime.

———————•———————

If you're inclined to do stuff like this, I hope you'll take the time to ask yourself whether or not whatever you're buying is a legitimate business expense or business investment. If it is, great. But if it isn't, what are you risking? Is it worth it?

If you don't have an expert who can answer those questions for you before you make your purchase, are you confident that you'll know what a reasonable business expense even looks like? If you take clients to a hockey game, and you spend a lot of time talking business, it's probably a legitimate business expense (but entertainment expenses like this are only 50 percent deductible). But if you decide to take your wife to that same game—or to London to see the World Cricket Final—it probably isn't.

If there's a one-day business event at a golf resort and you decide to spend a week there, your company can likely pick up the tab for the day of the event—one-seventh of your hotel stay. The other six days are likely yours personally (and the golf expenditures are specifically not deductible as set out in the Income Tax Act). If you decide to deduct all seven days, you're not just playing golf. You're playing audit roulette.

On several occasions, I have been invited to speak before groups on cruise ships, and I remember one conference where the organizers said in their marketing materials that participants could deduct some or all of their cost, including airfare. Well, they can say it, but that doesn't make it true. What if they're wrong? If you decide you can write the whole thing off because the organizers said you could, do you think they're going to pay your interest and penalties, in addition to the taxes you should have paid in the first place, if the auditors say otherwise?

Yes, it's possible that you can deduct some or even all of your trip—but there's no guarantee. Maybe you think it's okay, and maybe your accountant says it's okay too. But if it turns out that it *isn't* okay, it's all on you.

If you're relying on your usual advisor to keep you out of trouble, to help you toe the line between tax avoidance and tax evasion, then you'll be wise to consult with a good tax specialist who knows the tax laws inside and out—because the government doesn't care if your usual advisor gives you bad advice. Ignorance doesn't fly in a court of law.

I've seen some people deduct a couple hundred thousand dollars' worth of furniture they put into their homes. Their accountants told them, "Oh, that two hundred thousand dollars in furniture? You're going to be meeting clients in your home, right? Let's depreciate that furniture. Let's take the position that that's a business asset." They listened, and they got burned because their advisors really didn't know the tax laws. In the end, they had to pay a lot more than they would have if they'd just paid their taxes properly in the first place.

Nobody should pay even a penny more than he owes in taxes, so you have every reason to be aggressive in your efforts to keep what's yours. But keep in mind that you're the one who's ultimately responsible for every tax decision you make.

It's your company's tax return. It's your personal tax return. If everything's on the up-and-up—if you're paying what you properly owe—you have nothing to worry about.

If you decide to be aggressive in your filing, that's fine. But please . . . don't be silly. Even if you have only a 3 percent chance of being audited, don't play audit roulette.

Don't set yourself up to pay far more than you should have, because now you owe interest and penalties on the taxes you didn't pay in the first place. Don't set yourself up to be double taxed, or even triple taxed because you messed up both your company and personal planning. And please don't think that because you probably won't get charged with tax evasion, your risk is worth it.

Keep in mind that you could still be assessed gross negligence penalties, which carry a penalty of 50 percent of the tax you should have paid—on top of the tax you should have paid—plus interest that compounds daily. In a short period of time, you could easily find yourself paying double what you owed in the first place.

And finally, ask yourself this: What's the value of a good night's sleep? Do you want to lie awake all night wondering if your tax affairs are a little too aggressive, or thinking that the government's going to catch you . . . that you set yourself up to pay huge penalties and interest and additional accounting and legal costs?

Maybe you don't care. Maybe you're very wealthy and can pay all those costs comfortably, and you're willing to accept the risk of an audit because you thrive on that sort of tension. Maybe you'll sleep like a baby. But if you're the kind of person who lies awake at night worrying about this sort of thing, why not avoid it in the first place?

Most importantly, why not work with tax specialists who know every bit of the tax laws backward and forward and can give you the advice you need to keep every penny you can and still stay on the straight and narrow? Don't play audit roulette. It's just not worth it. It's silly.

CHAPTER 5

Fairness, Certainty, Convenience, and Economy

Let me tell you how it will be
There's one for you, nineteen for me
'Cause I'm the taxman
Yeah, I'm the taxman

Those are the opening lyrics of the song "Taxman," the first track on the Beatles' *Revolver* album. I'm bringing up that song because it was a solid-gold hit in 1966 . . . which coincidentally was the last time Canada took a serious look at its tax statute: the Income Tax Act (the "Tax Act").

That's right—our tax system has remained essentially the same for half a century. (Will you still need it, will you still feed it, when it's sixty-four?)

We've made some changes to the Tax Act over the years, but they've been incremental. Over time, it's become a patchwork quilt of amendments that even the best tax specialists have trouble comprehending.

And it's long past time we did something about it.

———————•———————

To understand how we got to where we are today, let's go back a century—to when the King of England, with the advice and consent of the Senate and House of Commons of Canada, enacted the Income War Tax Act of 1917.

It was Canada's first income tax, and it was intended to be temporary. The law was enacted to help pay for our involvement in World War I, and it was supposed to be swept into the dustbin of history when the war was over.

But, of course, that never happened. When "the war to end all wars" was finally over, and the time had come to toss the law aside, it had already become too heavy to lift off our shoulders. So we kept it, and it's been getting heavier ever since. Today, the income tax is Canada's largest source of revenue.

The Tax Act remained essentially unchanged for forty-five years, until Ottawa decided it was time to take a good, hard look at how it was taxing us. In 1962, Prime Minister John Diefenbaker appointed a group called the Royal Commission on Taxation—more commonly known as the Carter Commission, for Kenneth Carter, the man who led it—to thoroughly review the Tax Act and recommend ways to improve it.

Four years later, in 1966—the same year the Beatles released "Taxman"—the Carter Commission came back with a report that recommended overhauling the law to make it less complicated, more efficient, and fairer for everyone.

The report filled six volumes, considerably more than the eleven pages that were needed to write the entire Tax Act half a century earlier. Its most controversial recommendation was to implement a capital gains tax. Up until then, income derived from capital gains had been nontaxable, but the Commission— based on Carter's proclamation that "a buck is a buck is a buck"—recommended that all capital gains income should be taxed going forward.

It took six years for our politicians to scrutinize every line and wrangle over all the Commission's recommendations, but at the end of the day, the report formed the basis for the comprehensive tax reform that Canada implemented in 1972.

As for capital gains, the government split the baby in half. Fifty percent of capital gains income would be taxed; the other half would be nontaxable.

That was nearly fifty years ago, and we haven't really changed much of anything since. We've passed countless amendments to fix some of the law's unintended consequences and to plug inappropriate planning—but we haven't done anything on a grand scale to respond to societal change since 1972.

And now our Tax Act has become a patchwork quilt. It was comfortable and warm when we bought it, but the fabric wore out years ago. Today, every time a hole appears, every time some stitching unravels, we throw a new patch onto the quilt and sew it back together again. And all those patches have made it way too heavy. It's not much of a quilt anymore. It's essentially crushing us, and it's time to replace it with a new one.

But where do we begin?

I suggest we start by recalling a guy who's even older than Paul McCartney—the Scottish philosopher Adam Smith, the "Father of Economics."

Should five percent appear too small
Be thankful I don't take it all
'Cause I'm the taxman
Yeah, I'm the taxman

In 1776, in his historically acclaimed book, *The Wealth of Nations*, Adam Smith introduced his four canons of taxation:

The Canon of Equality. A good tax system should levy taxes fairly. The amount a citizen pays should be based on his ability to pay, and the wealthy should pay more than the poor.

The Canon of Certainty. Taxation should be objective, not subject to an official's whim. All citizens should know the exact amount they have to pay, how they are expected to pay it, and when their payment is due.

The Canon of Convenience. In order to avoid tax evasion and corruption, taxes should be citizen-friendly—easy to pay, levied in the most convenient manner, and payable at the most convenient time for the taxpayer.

The Canon of Economy. Because the goal of taxation is to provide services for the common good, the cost of collecting taxes should be as low as possible in order to keep net revenue high.

Smith laid out these guidelines for fair taxation a quarter of a millennium ago, but they're as relevant today as they were then. When I look at the state of Canada's tax system, I'm amazed to see how far we've strayed from our good intentions.

The tax system we have today is unequal, uncertain, inconvenient, and overly expensive. It simply isn't the tax system we should want. We've been patching the quilt for too long, and it's time to start looking for a new one.

We're long overdue for another Carter Commission.

———————

You may be reading this and thinking, *Hey, I'm okay with the way things are. I get a paycheck every week, my employer deducts my taxes, I fill out my forms on April 30, and that's the end of it.*

Well, for you, maybe it is.

Or maybe it isn't. Maybe you're actually paying less than you should, or maybe you're paying more.

Or maybe you really don't know. In fact, there's a very good chance that even your accountant, if you use one, really doesn't know—because the myriad rules and regulations we've piled onto the Tax Act have become incomprehensible.

Maybe you're not paying the correct tax on your capital gains. Maybe you think you're taking advantage of Canada's income-splitting provisions, but you're not doing it correctly. And maybe—indeed, probably—you don't know where or how to find out whether you are or aren't.

The rules are just too complex—not only for taxpayers, but for tax advisors and auditors too. And how can we expect the government to administer the rules fairly when even its own auditors have trouble understanding them?

An auditor may come to you and say the government is reassessing you because you're not playing by the rules. You'll reply that you've read the rules, you've consulted with a good advisor, and you most definitely are.

Then, after a lot of back and forth, he'll come back and say that his decision is final, and if you don't like it, then you have the right to go to appeal, and if you lose that appeal, go to court and let a judge decide. And now you're going to pay a lot of money and waste a lot of your time, even if it turns out that you were right.

Remember Adam Smith's Four Canons? Is this fair? Is this certain? Is this convenient? Is this economical?

We're supposed to be striving to satisfy all four canons, and we're oh-for-four.

<hr />

If you drive a car, I'll tax the street
If you try to sit, I'll tax your seat
If you get too cold, I'll tax the heat
If you take a walk, I'll tax your feet

It's clearly time for a change. But before we start reinventing the wheel, I strongly recommend reconsidering some modifications that were suggested in the past—by none other than the Carter Commission.

One recommendation the Commission made was to abandon our practice of taxing all citizens as individuals. As an alternative, it suggested treating married/common-law couples as single units to be taxed.

This is how income taxes are levied in many countries, including the United States, where a married couple can combine their income and file a single joint tax return.

The downside of doing this is . . . well, I don't think there really is one.

The government and some economists like to say that countries around the world are abandoning family taxation, and that some studies have shown that it hinders women who want to enter the workforce. But that's just plain nonsense. Just look to the south. The United States has had family taxation for decades, and the last time I looked, it wasn't holding back any woman who wanted to work.

So I don't see a downside; I see a big upside. Right now, a married or common-law couple in Canada has to combine their income in order to receive specific entitlements or to obtain certain tax credits—but they have to report their income separately and file separate tax returns. And because they can't just combine their income for the purpose of reducing their overall taxation, they try to make use of income-splitting "planning."

But the effect of all of this is that they wind up paying their accountant or tax advisor to assist them with income splitting; and then they pay them to prepare two tax returns instead of one.

That's a lot of paying and some mischief—and it's all because we don't allow couples to combine their income and file a single joint tax return.

That's just silly. We should have listened to the Carter Commission and rewritten the Tax Act to allow family taxation in 1972. But better late than never. The time has come to overhaul the law and get it right.

There are many other problems that need to be addressed, including the unfortunate fact that our Tax Act wasn't written to deal with some circumstances that were unimaginable fifty years ago.

Take the internet. The Carter Commission couldn't anticipate such a thing, but now we buy and sell just about anything and everything through smartphones, laptops, tablets, and desktop computers.

We're not quite certain how to tax all these transactions though. If you live in Toronto and you buy a pack of gum from a warehouse in Fiji, does the province of Ontario get to tax you? Does Canada? Does Fiji? What if the warehouse in Fiji is owned and operated by a company based in Seattle? These are all great questions that countries around the world are struggling with. The Organisation for Economic Co-operation and Development (OECD) is also struggling to provide answers to member countries on how taxation systems should be developed to address such challenges.

You also won't find the answers to these questions anywhere in the six volumes of the Carter Commission's report, because back then, anything even resembling the internet was the far-fetched stuff of science fiction novels.

But now it's here, and these questions are real. And they have to be addressed.

Don't ask me what I want it for
If you don't want to pay some more
'Cause I'm the taxman
Yeah, I'm the taxman

We've mentioned Paul McCartney and Adam Smith. Now let's talk about another old guy you may have heard of—an astrophysicist named Albert Einstein.

Einstein once said, "This is too difficult for a mathematician. It takes a philosopher. The hardest thing in the world to understand is the income tax."

He was right. I think mastering the theory of relativity is a good way to warm up your brain before you tackle our Tax Act. I sometimes wonder how anyone can file a correct tax return if they can't even explain quantum physics.

But why should understanding the Tax Act be so hard—especially when it's so important to all of us? We shouldn't hate paying taxes, and we shouldn't dread filing our returns. We should embrace doing those things because taxes provide the government with the money it needs to serve us. If we don't pay taxes, we can't repair our roads. We can't maintain our electric grid. We can't fund our law enforcers and armed forces. We can't pay for education and health care and other important social services.

If you're the sort of person who doesn't care about what the government provides, I think you should rethink that. But if you do that, and you still don't care, I'll give you one more reason why you should. You have the right to be selfish. Taxes are the number one depleter of your income. They're sucking money out of your till every minute of every day—so you really should care about how much you're paying and where your money is going.

It's your money, and the government is taking it from you—so if you want to increase your wealth, you should care about how much money you're giving away and what's happening to it when it's gone. You should care that the Tax Act's radically out of whack, because maybe you'll feel better about paying taxes if your government does something to straighten it out—and maybe you'll pay less.

———————•———————

Fixing things won't be too hard if we care enough to do it and eliminate politics that stand in the way (yes, that's much easier said than done).

Many economists, accountants, lawyers, and government bureaucrats will tell you that comprehensive tax reform/review is a terrible idea or that Canadians are not ready—but that's mostly because the current system works for them. For example, the whole concept of tax splitting creates more work for accountants.

The government clamped down on income splitting in 2017 because the perception was that it was being widely abused, but the net effect was to make the rules dramatically more complex than they were before. And that's just wrong—because it's one thing to have complex rules that target a small group of people who can afford to pay for tax advice, but it's a whole other thing when you create rules that are virtually incomprehensible and can apply to everyone.

You can't enact rules like this with little or no thought about their impact on average taxpayers and their advisors. That's just wrong. If a new rule can't adhere to the Canon of Certainty, then dump it in the trash, and devise a better one.

There's absolutely no reason why the average taxpayer—the man or woman who works for a company and gets paid a regular salary—should have to hire an accountant or tax advisor to help with their tax returns. Make the Tax Act fair, make it simple, and make the accountants and advisors limit their services to people whose tax formulations are more complex.

In 2017, I traveled to Ottawa to meet with—among other people—some government bureaucrats to discuss some of the new rules and regulations that were affecting my clients. I'm pretty friendly with a lot of them, so there was nothing unusual about one of them pulling me aside to chat.

He asked me, "So, Kim, what do you think of these rules?"

"They're horrible," I told him.

"What do you mean?" he said. "They'll create more business for you. You should be happy."

Well, I wasn't happy. I was surprised by such a statement. There's a prevailing attitude among people in general that tax complexity drives business to my profession, so there's no reason why people like me should advocate for positive change.

And that's offensive. I think the better people in my profession—and there's a lot of them—want the government to make things simpler for our clients, and Canadians in general, so they can plan their affairs without having to rely on us so much.

"Oh, but won't that mean less business for you, Kim?"

Yes, it will. And you know what? That will be a positive thing for our country, because people shouldn't need people like me to help them navigate routine stuff. If they could do more stuff themselves, I'd have more time and be more available to help my clients navigate the really tough stuff.

I don't want the simple stuff. Taxpayers should be able to do it themselves. They shouldn't need people like me to help them.

The next thing we need to do is take a hard look at our government's revenue sources and carefully consider whether such revenue sources need reform, expansion, or elimination. This includes giving serious consideration to the question of whether we need an income tax at all.

If it were up to me, I'd get rid of the income tax (or, at a minimum, significantly reduce its application) and replace it with a consumption tax—because I believe that a "progressive" tax system that imposes increasingly higher tax rates on increasingly higher income levels can be counterproductive.

Progressives argue that it's fair to expect the wealthy to pay a higher percentage of their income in taxes, but I believe there's a point at which it becomes unfair—not only to the wealthy, but to everyone.

In 1974, the American economist Arthur Laffer sat down at a luncheon with some of President Gerald Ford's high-level staffers, and he famously drew a diagram on a paper napkin to demonstrate why he believed that a proposed increase in tax rates would not increase revenue, as Ford's advisors were claiming it would.

The diagram, which became known as the Laffer Curve, showed that when the government increases taxes on businesses, those businesses become more inclined to find ways to save the money that remains and less likely to invest it in new ventures that would boost the economy.

Likewise, Laffer said, the more tax money you take from workers, the less inclined they are to do hard work.

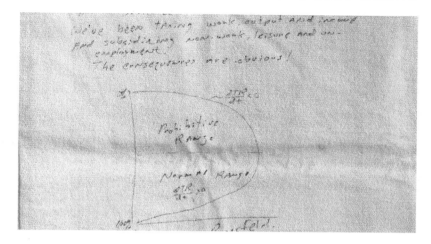

Seven years later, Laffer's theory of supply-side economics became the foundation of President Ronald Reagan's tax policy, which led to one of the biggest tax cuts in US history.

To this day there's a lot of debate about whether Laffer was right—but I'm still sitting in his corner. I believe taxpayer behavior changes when tax rates increase to a certain level, and that governments actually collect less revenue when they push the rate too high. And recent history suggests I'm right.

In 2015, Prime Minister Justin Trudeau announced his intention to tax the wealthy "just a little bit more"—but when the law went into effect on January 1, 2016, that little bit turned out to be 4 percent more on personal income in excess of $200,000.

With the tax increase now on the books, the Department of Finance budgeted $3.2 billion that it expected to collect—but things didn't turn out the way they'd planned. Instead of increasing its revenue, the government wound up taking in $4.6 billion *less* in 2016.

Well played, Ottawa.

I believe Arthur Laffer knew what he was talking about. When you raise the tax rate too high, you end up inhibiting growth. But that doesn't mean we should do nothing. I've been saying for years—along with many economists—that ditching the income tax and replacing it with a consumption tax will result in a huge boost for our economy.

A consumption tax is like a value-added tax. You pay taxes based on how much you spend, not on how much you earn.

Let's say you're in the market for a car, and you're going to pay a sales tax of 15 percent. You can buy a Kia for $20,000 and pay $3,000 in tax. You can buy a Tesla for $60,000 and pay $9,000 in tax. You can buy a Maserati for $300,000 and pay $45,000 in tax. The more you spend, the more you're taxed.

People say it's unfair to apply the same tax rate to everyone, but the fact is that everyone buys differently.

Yes, a multibillionaire who chooses not to spend money for anything but the bare necessities won't pay more in taxes than a guy making $40,000 a year—but that's just because he's chosen not to enjoy the perks of earning all that money.

I tend to think that won't happen. I think he'll want to buy expensive stuff . . . because he can. Everyone wants more toys, and the multibillionaire is lucky—he can have all the toys he wants. He'll just have to pay more in taxes to have them.

Now, there are those who will say it's still unfair, that even the most frugal multibillionaire should have to pay more in taxes than a guy who works on the assembly line and has to support a wife and four kids. I can't argue with that—but I don't think we have to fiddle with a consumption tax-based system to help him. A well-designed consumption-based tax code could carve out some basic exemptions to help people who need assistance. There's nothing wrong with the government lending a hand to those who need it. There's no reason we can't all pay the same consumption tax and agree to dispatch some of the revenue it creates to people who need it.

And there just might be more money in the till to provide that help—because adopting a consumption tax and eliminating the income tax would remove the disincentive to earn more if it's going to push you into a higher tax bracket.

Finally, there's one more thing we need to do: We need to stop demonizing wealthy individuals and businesses that have committed the heinous crime of being successful. We have to stop presuming that wealthy people are all extortionists, and that they're determined to exploit others simply because they have money.

We need to stop doing this because, at the end of the day, people who are wealthy—unless they're trust-fund babies—have built their businesses and earned their fortunes through hard work, careful investment, and selective risk.

That's the foundation of our capitalist society, so hooray for them. If you work hard and take calculated risks, you may be successful. And if you succeed, and you keep succeeding, you can create jobs for the rest of us.

Twenty-five years ago, I decided to deploy my entrepreneurial juices, and along with my partners, we opened our own shop. We took some calculated risks, and we've been very successful. We've grown to the point that we now employ about sixty people.

Now, if we hadn't taken those risks, and if we hadn't been successful, there'd be sixty fewer jobs available for our fellow Canadians.

When you demonize the rich, when you stifle their determination to take risks, when you tax them more and more, all you're doing is giving them lots of reasons not to work so hard.

We have a serious problem of poverty in our country, and it's something we have to deal with. But when you demonize the rich indiscriminately, you're attacking a lot of wealthy people who are creating jobs for others. That's called biting the hand that feeds you. Keep it up, and you'll wind up hungry.

Now my advice for those who die
Declare the pennies on your eyes
'Cause I'm the taxman
Yeah, I'm the taxman
And you're working for no one but me

CHAPTER 6

It Shouldn't Be the Practitioners versus the Bureaucrats

The Department of Finance Canada helps the Government of Canada develop and implement strong and sustainable economic, fiscal, tax, social, security, international, and financial sector policies and programs.

Those aren't my words. They're how the Department of Finance describes its role in Canadian society, right at the top of its government website. It exists to help the government develop and implement. That's its job.

In the 2017 federal budget, the Department of Finance announced that it planned to release a consultation paper laying out in detail a series of changes it wanted to make to the tax rules for private corporations and their shareholders. The department listed three issues it intended to address: income splitting, taxation of private income in a corporation, and surplus stripping—how business owners take surplus money out of their companies.

When tax advisors, including me, saw that announcement, we thought, "Okay, we'll wait for them to release the consultation paper, and we'll see what they have to say." We were pleased that they were calling it a consultation paper because we interpreted that to mean that the department was planning to consult and possibly even collaborate with us before it introduced any new laws.

We thought that made a lot of sense since we're the ones who advise taxpayers and help them file their taxes. We'd be able to help the government develop and implement the policies and programs that affect our clients. The Department of Finance was smart to welcome our input.

Well, that's what we thought. But that's not what happened.

For more than a hundred years, ever since the government started collecting income tax, there has been tension between the bureaucrats who administer the tax laws and the practitioners who help businesses and individuals determine how much they owe and how to minimize how much they pay.

The tension comes naturally, because the system is designed to breed distrust. The government expects taxpayers to self-assess their individual tax obligations and to pay that amount no later than April 30. In other words, we, the taxpayers—not the bureaucrats—calculate how much we owe.

The government expects us to be honest and cooperative—but, just in case, it retains the right to review our math and filing positions to make sure we're good citizens. And, of course, it has a cadre of auditors ready to pounce if it thinks we're holding back.

All of this would be unnecessary, of course, if the government calculated our taxes for us and sent us an honest and accurate invoice for payment. Or if it eliminated income taxation entirely and replaced it with a consumption tax that applied equally to everyone.

But don't hold your breath, expecting either of those solutions to happen soon. For the time being, the bureaucrats will continue to expect taxpayers to cooperate with them.

There's a big problem with this arrangement. The Income Tax Act is frightfully complicated for taxpayers who aren't employees—for those whose income doesn't come from a regular salary. It's incomprehensible to the point that they have to rely on advisors—practitioners—to help them wade through the arcane language and figure out how much they owe.

That makes practitioners a vital cog in the tax system, a key component to ensuring that everything runs smoothly—but the bureaucrats don't always see it that way. Or, at least, they don't always act like they do. They sure didn't see it in 2017.

The relationship between the bureaucrats and the practitioners has had its ups and downs over the decades. There will always be some level of disagreement because the tax administrators will never fully trust the taxpayers to file honestly and accurately, and because taxpayers will always look for every possible way to minimize how much they legally must pay. As such, a degree of friction is natural—but sometimes things get out of hand.

I've been told that the two sides were engaged in what was practically an all-out war before the 1980s, and that it wasn't until the early '90s that the two sides called a truce and decided to work together to bridge the gap. Things settled down for a while after that, but the armistice was too good to last. Now the gap has widened again.

In 2017, after the Department of Finance announced its plan to propose changes to the Tax Act in a consultation letter, the bureaucrats proceeded to draft legislation for two of the three consultation points without getting any input—absolutely none whatsoever—from the practitioners who advise taxpayers and help file their tax returns. There was no consultation, and there was no consideration given to how the practitioners felt the proposals would affect their clients.

That's just not how things are supposed to be done. There will always be a degree of friction between the bureaucrats and the practitioners—but their confrontation should be a healthy give-and-take, like a spirited but friendly game of chess. It should not be an all-out war.

But in 2017, the politicians, assisted by the bureaucrats, declared war. They extended their arm and swept all the pieces right off the chessboard.

———————•———————

The Department of Finance ministry and bureaucrats fired the first shot on July 18, 2017—five months after they announced their plan to release a consultation paper. It was the middle of summer, and I was on vacation in Niagara-on-the-Lake, a gorgeous spot on the shores of Lake Ontario, very close to Niagara Falls. I was walking down the street with my family when my phone blew up—it started buzzing and ringing, and it wouldn't stop.

The Department of Finance had just announced that it had released its consultation paper, and it was starting the clock on a seventy-six-day period to discuss the proposed changes to the Tax Act that were in it.

There was, indeed, a consultation paper. But it came with an attachment, something much more serious than a mere proposal. It was draft legislation to deal with two of the three pillars—income splitting and surplus stripping—that the department had said it wanted to review. The third pillar—taxation of passive income inside a private corporation—was addressed in the consultation paper, but no legislation had been drafted to deal with it.

Now, take a minute to think about what all that meant. First of all, draft legislation is not consultation. Consultation is supposed to take place *before* you draft legislation. Draft legislation shows policy intent and a clear legislative intent to change the Tax Act. The Department of Finance had announced that it would host a hundred-yard dash, and now it was starting the race just a few feet from the finish line.

It should have released a consultation paper and said, "Here . . . have a look. This is what we believe needs to be fixed. Here's what we'd like to do. Now tell us: What do you think?" —but the ministry and bureaucrats skipped all of that. They went straight to the finish line and released draft legislation.

That legislation included some of the most complex stuff I've ever seen—and to make things worse, they gave us seventy-six days to "consult." It was July 18, and they were giving us until October 2.

Now, they may have thought that they were giving us a lot of time to consider their proposal, but they really weren't because this happened in the summer, when most practitioners take their vacations. And when we get back from vacation in late August, it's time to get our kids back to school.

Seventy-six days may be sufficient time to react slowly and deliberately in the fall, winter, or spring. But in the middle of summer, it's anything but adequate. This was a fire drill—a purposeful, disingenuous attempt to ram very significant changes in the tax statute down the throats of a sleeping public.

The Department of Finance was proposing to make substantial changes to items in the Tax Act that had been essentially unchanged for fifty years. Seventy-six days wasn't nearly enough time for "consulting" on measures this consequential—especially in the summer.

The 2017 "consultation paper" marked a turning point in the relationship between the ministry and bureaucrats who administer taxes—and the practitioners who represent the taxpayers. It was an affront to the taxpayer community, and the practitioners did not take it lying down.

Our reaction was, "Oh, you wanna play ball? You wanna ram this down people's throats, without genuine consultation and with no interest at all in what's gonna happen when the rubber hits the road? You think you're just gonna foist this stuff on us? No way you're getting away with that."

And that was just the opening salvo. Things went downhill from there.

The Department of Finance was proposing some very technical changes that obviously had been sitting in the hopper for some time—until a prime minister came along who was willing to support them and drive them through. When Justin Trudeau became prime minister in 2015, be bought into the whole Occupy mentality that big business is inherently bad and that business owners are all cheaters.

Well, that didn't go over very well. It was a terrible situation, and the tax community hit back pretty hard. Once they realized the drastic nature of the department's proposals, they forgot all about the season. They stopped fishing and started fighting. There were twenty-one thousand submissions made to the Department of Finance in response to its consultation paper.

The media hit back pretty hard too. Suddenly, taxes were front and center, above the fold on Canadian newspapers practically every day for four months. It was *the* news story, the subject of numerous articles and op-eds from mid-August until mid-December—and almost all those stories and editorials were highly critical of the government because taxpayers felt slighted and insulted.

The ministry and bureaucrats got killed in the press, and ultimately, they backed down and withdrew and/or watered down many of their proposals. They had no choice; they were being portrayed as sloppy.

The draft legislation was probably the sloppiest technical package I've ever seen. It was rife with errors. It was more than horribly insulting; it was embarrassing. It didn't exit gently or quietly though.

As co-chair of the Joint Committee on Taxation between the Chartered Professional Accountants of Canada and the Canadian Bar Association, I cosigned a massive submission to the Department of Taxation on October 2 in response to its proposals.

One day later, on October 3, the Trudeau government started making announcements about how the proposals were progressing. A couple of weeks after that, it felt like Christmastime came early that year. Santa Claus kept coming to town, making a new announcement every day.

One special day, the minister of finance and the prime minister showed up at a pizza shop and announced that they were going to proceed with the income-splitting proposals. They said they would be taking into consideration all the comments they'd heard and that they would be releasing simplified proposals before the end of fall.

And sure enough, they finally did. On December 13—the very last day that Parliament was in session—they released a set of revised proposals that were better, but only slightly. They were still incredibly complex.

That was no way to make any policy, let alone something as complex as tax policy. It was a blatant attempt by the ministry and certain government bureaucrats to ram through tax policy changes without any input from its constituents. I hope we never see anything like it again.

I hope our politicians will be smart enough in the future to remember that boondoggle, and that any new attempts to introduce draft legislation—especially when it's so pervasive and complex—will be proposed at a time when the practitioner community can actually study the text and provide meaningful input.

Today, because of what happened in 2017, the relationship between the bureaucrats and the practitioners has cycled back to a lower point. My colleagues and I are very skeptical now about what's going on at the top level of our government.

The Department of Finance's proposals were antibusiness and far left of center, and they found a sympathetic ear in Ottawa that never would have listened if Trudeau hadn't been prime minister. For the antibusiness bureaucrats, it was a confluence of good timing: a left-of-center government came into power, bringing with it a collection of politicians who wanted to impose their liberal agenda.

There's nothing inherently wrong or unusual about that. It's the normal give-and-take of political philosophy that's part of a democratic society. But no matter which side of the political fence you live on, you're supposed to go through proper channels. And a genuine consultation of affected constituents is part of that channel.

In 2017, however, our political leaders decided to skip that step. They decided they'd just rewrite the rules and sneak them through in the summer while everyone was napping.

They tried to make it look good by giving people seventy-six days to reply—but they knew that wasn't nearly enough. They knew what they were really doing. They knew because, in any season, it takes much more than seventy-six days to effect significant changes in tax law. Don't forget—the last time we had major tax review/reform, it took *four years* to get it done.

And make no mistake about it: those proposed changes were major. The bureaucrats were trying to rewrite significant and foundational portions of the Tax Act—especially as it related to surplus stripping and the taxation of passive income. There's a time-honored process that's supposed to be followed— and they went to great lengths to avoid following it.

———————•———————

Good government is supposed to be transparent. That means you have an obligation to reach out to everyone who will be affected. It means engaging the taxpayers. It means consulting with practitioners and academics and economists. It means reaching out to work together, not forcing your ideas down the taxpayers' throats.

It means going to Parliament, putting through a bill, and being patient—because if it takes four years or more, that's how our system is supposed to work. You don't just come in and say, "Never mind all that; we want what we want, we want it now, and we don't care how we get it."

It means doing things right, because when you try to force your will on people, they're less likely to cooperate. They're more likely to look at what you're doing and decide that they can't trust you and they're not going to pay their taxes. And if that were to happen, it would be a disaster—because, as I said earlier, taxation in Canada is a self-assessing system. The government is depending on us, the taxpayers, to determine how much we owe and to pay that amount in a timely fashion. If they want us to play by the rules, then they have to play by them too.

What happened in 2017 was a war, not a chess match. I can only hope that our country will learn from what it went through and that it will do better next time.

CHAPTER 7

Anyone Can Say, "I Can Do Your Taxes"— So Buyer, Beware

et's say you're an accountant. Seriously, let's just say it, since in Canada, if you want to call yourself an accountant, nobody's going to stop you—because nobody can.

You can't practice medicine without a medical degree. You can't practice law without a law degree. You can't even cut someone's hair without a barber's license. But if you want to practice accountancy in Canada, all you have to do is say you're an accountant. Education, certification, accreditation . . . all optional. They're nice, but they're not required. Just say you're an accountant, and you're an accountant.

I'm an accountant. I've been working in the field for more than twenty-five years, and not once during my career has our government passed a law or imposed any sort of regulation that compels me to prove I know what I'm doing. And that's appalling because millions of taxpayers from Yukon to

Newfoundland depend on accountants to help them file accurate tax returns—and, according to the law, anyone can tell them to look no further; they've found the guy they're looking for.

It sounds crazy, but that's the way it is. There is nothing in Canada that requires the "professionals" most people pay to help them with their taxes to know anything about our country's tax statute. They can say they're tax specialists even if they're not—and most of them are not.

I've spent a lot of time in the last twenty-five years cleaning up messes—from simple errors to flat-out fraud—that so-called accountants created for their clients because they weren't qualified to handle even their own taxes, let alone someone else's.

They said they knew what they were doing. They bragged about their tax expertise. And then their clients found out, way too late, that they were actually clueless about tax law, or—even worse—that they were frauds.

So, if you're seeking help in doing your taxes, keep this in mind: Most accountants aren't tax experts. They're bean counters. That's a derisive term, but it really shouldn't be because millions of people need help counting their beans, and accountants are really good at it. They're great at balancing ledgers and keeping track of every dollar that goes in and out—but very few of them know the intricate details of Canada's Tax Act.

I think most accountants, if they're honest, will tell you they agree. They're not really tax experts, but some tell the public they are. And they do it because tax sells. Taxpayers need help filing their tax returns, and accountants generate business by saying they're up to the job—even when they know they're not.

The ins and outs of the Tax Act really should be the domain of lawyers because the job involves interpreting statutes and giving advice. But lawyers—in general—aren't interested in helping people with their taxes. Even if they were, there are not a lot of tax lawyers in Canada, and therefore, there are not nearly enough of them to handle all the work. So the job, by default, has landed in the laps of accountants, some of whom are very unqualified.

That's why we Canadians are long overdue for some government regulation of what accountants are, what they do, and what the minimum qualifications should be for them to say they can do it.

You're looking for a tax expert because you work hard for your money, and you want to keep as much of it as you legally can.

Enter the accountants. They know what you're looking for, so they make it their selling point. They'll tell you they know every loophole and every deduction out there, and they'll put on their creative hats, interpret the tax laws, and give you solid advice. Maybe there once was a time when most accountants could do that, but that time is long gone. Over the last decade or so—and especially in the last three or four years—tax law has become so complex, even full-time tax-specialist accountants/lawyers have a hard time figuring it out.

This has created a perfect storm: a glut of complex legislation, too few true tax-specialist accountants/lawyers, no rules or regulations to rein in accountants who call themselves tax experts or tax specialists, and some accountants who are not willing to acknowledge their limitations and seek help from experts when they can't interpret the law. We're in a confused marketplace, and the people who are affected most are the consumers of tax services—just about everyone whose income doesn't come from a salary.

I don't worry about all of them. I know the big consumers of tax services will get good advice because they can afford to seek out the best tax experts in the business. I worry—a lot—about the small to midsize taxpayers, the ones who need advice and either don't know where to get it or think they're already getting it from advisors who say they're tax experts but really aren't.

And this is why I strongly believe it's time to establish official, nationwide standards for accountants and tax experts.

———•———

This was not an easy decision for me. I've always thought that the best market is a free market, and I tend to be wary of government regulation, but I've come to the conclusion that it's long past time for accountants and lawyers to acknowledge that their clients need to be certain that their tax experts really are experts.

And I believe the only way to make that happen is to establish standard tax designations and tax specializations that can be achieved through rigorous study and continuous education. Just as physicians study for years before being awarded degrees or acknowledged specializations that establish their competence, accountants and lawyers who offer tax advice should have to prove that they've studied and practiced in their field and have kept themselves current with the tax statute.

A certificate of competency won't do anything for an old-timer like me who has years of experience and has earned a reputation that's better than any degree. But this isn't about me. This is about the consumers and the youngsters who are entering the profession. I think it helps consumers to know that their young advisors have invested a lot of time and money to learn and understand the tax statute, that they're not just somebody with an office and a shingle hanging outside the door.

Several years ago, I took part in an (ultimately futile) effort by the Canadian Tax Foundation to establish something similar to the United Kingdom's Chartered Tax Advisor qualification, which students can receive only after they've completed seven exams in two to three years, followed by three years of professional experience. Ireland and Australia have similar programs. Canada doesn't, for no apparent reason. But it's long past time it did.

We tried, and we failed, but I still maintain that a chartered tax advisor designation in Canada would help protect taxpayers from accountants who don't know or understand our Tax Act, and from fraudsters who deliberately run afoul of it.

———————

I've laid out the case for having a tax-specialization system that protects Canada's taxpayers. But, sadly, I think it will be a while before our nation adopts one. In the meantime, it's up

ɔayers to be more selective of whom they choose to help
.... devise their tax strategies and prepare their returns.

They need to ask their practitioners how much they know
about taxes, where they acquired their knowledge, how long
they've been in practice, and how many clients they have helped
in their careers.

They should demand that their practitioners have, at the
very least, completed some tax courses in their undergradu-
ate studies, and that they've gone through CPA Canada's In-
Depth Tax Program, a roughly three-year program run by the
Chartered Professional Accountants of Canada.

If they choose a tax lawyer and not an accountant, they
should make sure that their lawyer received the necessary education, either in law school or in an LLM program.

Once they determine that their practitioner has had the
proper education, that becomes the starting point for even
more questions:

Have you continued to practice as a tax advisor?

Do you spend at least 80 percent of your time practicing
in tax?

You do? Great. Let's continue.

You don't? Then what do you do for ongoing tax education?

You take a couple of courses once a year? Do you think
that's enough?

You have to ask these questions because you can't just rely
on what the practitioner has put on his website. Even bumbling
incompetents and fraudsters look awesome on their websites.

You need to dig further, because the CRA will ultimately
hold *you* responsible for any mistakes in your tax filings. If you

pay too little, the government will expect you—not your practitioner—to come up with what you still owe. And if you pay too much, your practitioner won't be out a penny; you'll be the one who's overpaid.

———————

Once you've decided to work with an accountant or a tax lawyer, your job isn't done. You should remain vigilant. Stay alert for red flags. If you hear something that sounds like an alarm, don't ignore it.

If you own a business, for example, and your advisor says it's okay to pay a salary to family members up to their personal tax exemptions—even if they aren't actively working for you—a siren should go off in your head. Because doing that is silly. The law will prevent your company from writing off the expense, but it still requires your family member to include the amount in his personal income. Classic double taxation. If you want to do this, and your advisor says it's okay, then you need to find a new advisor.

Another example is if you're trying to claim personal expenses as deductible business expenses. Your practitioner might ask if you went on any vacations in the last year and if you talked business during them. If you say you did, and he suggests deducting the trip as a business expense, then, once again, it's time to find a new advisor. Because that isn't tax brilliance. That might even be tax evasion.

The same applies if you're trying to deduct an expensive meal with your spouse in a fancy restaurant, or a couple's massage at the health spa on a so-called business cruise. Or if you say you have a home office and you write off part of your mortgage interest and property taxes and insurance and utilities—but you really don't do very much business in there.

Here's the bottom line: if it isn't business, it isn't deductible. That kind of stuff is common, but it shouldn't be—because it's flat-out wrong and it cheats the majority of taxpayers who don't do it. So, if your practitioner says it's okay, go ahead and declare it as a business expense anyway because you're very unlikely to get caught—you need a better practitioner.

Maybe you *will* get away with it. Maybe you *won't* get audited. But what if you do? What if you *do* get caught doing that kind of stuff? If that happens, you'll be forced to pay much more than you would have paid if you hadn't done it in the first place. So if your so-called tax expert is advising you to do it, find a new practitioner.

I have a lot of sympathy for some people who listen to advisors like that. Maybe they really don't know, or maybe they think their advisor would never give them bad advice—or maybe their advisor thinks he knows what he's talking about, but he really doesn't. But I have no sympathy at all for people who actually do know, or who should have known, and just went along with the practitioner's advice to avoid paying what they owed.

If you're smart and well educated and have a lot of business experience, and your accountant tells you, "Hey, I've got a way that I can get all your taxes back. All we have to do is claim some deductions that I promise you are allowed, because I've been doing this for years," do you just go along for the ride, or do you ask the obvious questions: "How come nobody else is doing this? How did you discover the secret sauce? How can you be the only smart guy in Canada?"

Don't ever forget that if it sounds too good to be true, it probably is. And if you go along with it, you're being willfully blind. If you get audited, you'll get no sympathy from me—because you knew better. I'll save my sympathy for the ones who didn't, the ones who didn't know their accountants were giving them bad tax advice.

I feel sorry for them because the tax collector doesn't hand out ignorance passes. If you get bad tax advice, and you do what you're told—even unknowingly—it's still on you if you get audited.

I wrote earlier in this chapter that tax sells, but it bears repeating because it's why most accountants will try to sell you on the notion that they know all about our Tax Act. Providing tax advice is an important part of their business, whether they're truly qualified or not, so they have to say they're up to the task.

But just because tax sells doesn't mean you should be buying. As crazy as it sounds, tax is an unregulated animal in Canada. Anyone can call himself an accountant and say he can do your taxes, so it's up to you to weed out the ones who really can't—no matter what they say.

I place tax-advising accountants into five categories:

1. **The competent competent.** These are accountants who are not only competent, but also know the Tax Act backward and forward and can offer sound advice.

2. **The competent incompetent.** This is the biggest group. These advisors are very good practitioners, and they know their limitations. If they're not competent enough to handle your tax needs, they'll bring in an expert who can do what they can't.

3. **The incompetent.** These advisors simply don't belong in the business. They're not good at what they do, and they know nothing about taxes.

4. **The incompetent competent.** These advisors recognize that tax sells, so they aren't up front with their clients when they know they're not up to the job.

5. **The incompetent incompetent.** These are the fraudsters, the ones who have no trepidations about dishing out bad advice and fleecing their clients.

Those last two categories—the incompetent competent and the incompetent incompetent—can severely hurt you. If you depend on them for tax advice and let them help you file your tax returns, you risk being audited and ultimately being forced to pay not only what you should have paid in the first place, but interest and penalties too.

But, you ask, what are the chances of that happening? That's a fair question. It's undeniably true that your chances of being audited are slim. Some state that only about 3 percent of taxpayers—one out of thirty-three—are flagged for a second look, so your odds are good if you're in the mood to play audit roulette.

But before you spin that wheel, think about this: just because you haven't been audited today doesn't mean you won't be in the future. All the CRA has done is process your return. There's nothing to stop it from looking more closely at it later.

If you think everything's fine because you haven't heard from the CRA, you're wrong. The taxman can go back and review your return anytime within three years from the original date of your notice of assessment—or more if it thinks you've misrepresented your situation due to carelessness or willful action, or if he thinks you've committed fraud.

But that's not all. It turns out that your chances of getting audited are likely much greater than 3 percent, because the vast majority of tax returns are "slip returns"—meaning there are T4 slips to support the taxpayer's declaration of income. Most returns fall into that category—and if they're not 100 percent accurate, they're awfully close. But in your case, when you're reporting business income or income that's tied to a private corporation and isn't documented on slips, chances are good that there are some debatable issues buried in your filing.

The people who get slip reports know their returns are accurate or just slightly off—but you're not so confident because you don't get a routine salary, and your filing is open to many more questions. Now, who do you think sleeps better at night— the guy whose slip return gets audited or the guy who runs a business?

There's one more reason that the 3 percent figure should give you no comfort at all. It's because you're playing audit roulette.

Let's talk about roulette. Let's say you step up to the roulette wheel and put your money on a single number—maybe the number nine, because if it was good enough for Gordie Howe, it's good enough for you. There are thirty-seven pockets on the roulette wheel, so if you put your money on just that one pocket, your odds of winning are one in thirty-seven. And the odds won't change, no matter how many times you spin the wheel. Keep playing just one number, and they'll be one in thirty-seven every time. You're savvy; you know this.

Here's another thing you know: sooner or later—maybe on the next spin, maybe next week—that ball will drop into the nine slot. The only thing you don't know is when. It's the same with tax roulette. Your odds against being audited are thirty-three to one, and they'll be thirty-three to one next year and the year after that.

But sooner or later, your turn will come. And when it does, if you've been underreporting or misreporting your tax obligation, your auditor will hand you a bill for not only what you failed to pay, but also for interest and penalties. And maybe your auditor will start to think, *Hey, I'll bet this guy did the same thing last year too . . . and the year before that.*

That's when you'll wish you'd had a tax practitioner who knew every nook and cranny of the Tax Act—in other words, a "competent competent" advisor.

Several years ago, a politician invited me to participate in a panel discussion in Alberta on some controversial tax law proposals. There were about three hundred people—mostly farmers, with a few small-business owners—in the room, and a local accountant and I were the scheduled speakers.

I gave a little lecture on what the rules were, and then it was the accountant's turn. It wasn't long before he went off the deep end, talking about stuff that wasn't even being proposed, like offshore taxes. He didn't have a clue about what he was talking about, but he was the local guy—the man those farmers and small businessmen were going to for tax advice.

I did what I could, nicely, to suggest to the attendees that he was out of his league, and that there might be some opinions worth considering that were different from his. I wanted to be polite, but I also wanted to make clear that this accountant should not be their advisor—because if there's one thing I've learned in all my years in business, it's that some advisors just aren't qualified to give advice.

Only a handful are actually criminals. Most of them just aren't up to the job. But they know that people will pay them to do it, and they have to make a living, and they don't have to be regulated, and they don't need a degree.

You need them, and they know they can hang a shingle outside their door, build an attractive website, and do the best they can. And if the best they can do isn't good enough, it's the customer's problem, not theirs.

Tax sells. That's a fact. And that's why a lot of practitioners hesitate to tell their clients, "Sorry, you're in the wrong place. I really don't know enough about tax." They're just not going to do that. It's bad for business.

In a better environment, they'd be able to tell their clients that they intend to do the best they can, and they're ready to bring in an expert to handle anything they can't. But we're not in that environment. For now—and for the foreseeable future—it's all too easy for an accountant or a lawyer to call himself a tax expert, and let the buyer beware.

Tax sells, and he's selling it. Whether or not you choose to buy is up to you.

CHAPTER 8

What Do the Wealthy Really Owe?

When it comes to running a business, no man or woman in the world does it worse than the government. The government can't create jobs efficiently; it is not a creator of wealth, and—worst of all—it loathes taking risks, which any entrepreneur will tell you is the key to success.

I learned this firsthand a couple of decades ago. I'm a wine enthusiast, and when I started pursuing that interest, every now and then I'd find myself speaking with Americans who had never been to Canada before. Many of them told me they'd walked into a liquor store in Ontario to buy a bottle of wine, and they were shocked—not only by the outrageously high prices, but also by the appallingly poor selection.

They were right on both counts. The cost was stratospheric, and the variety was drastically limited because the liquor stores in Ontario were government controlled. The province chose what wines could be sold and how much they cost. That was good for the government—the liquor stores were a good income generator—but it wasn't good at all for people who liked to drink wine.

But the scenario was very different a couple thousand miles to the west, in Alberta, where the provincial government proposed in the early 1990s that they get out of the liquor business and let the private sector run it instead.

It took a bit of a fight to make it happen. There were doomsday prophets who said the next thing you'd know, everyone would be staggering around in an alcoholic stupor—but sober minds prevailed. The province still got a nice slice of the pie—it made a pile of money from application, distribution, and licensing fees and taxes on all sales. But the liquor stores themselves were owned and operated by private entities.

And what happened then? It wasn't long before Alberta's liquor stores had some of the best wine selections in Canada. And nearly thirty years later, they still do. I see the difference every time I go to Ontario. I can't get what I want—or even something comparable to what I want—because there's no free market there. If the government doesn't sell it, you just can't buy it.

That's the difference between government control and entrepreneurship. Entrepreneurs are much better at the business of doing business.

———•———

There's no escaping the fact that our government needs a source of income. If you like having law enforcers to protect us, having teachers to educate us, having firefighters to protect our homes and our forests, having road crews to maintain our highways, if you think maintaining a military is a pretty good idea and so on, then you know why we need to fund their employer—the government.

But that doesn't mean we shouldn't keep a watchful eye on how the government generates its income. If it's mindlessly doing what it has always done simply because it can't be bothered to consider alternatives, then it may well be wasting money to make money. And that should concern all of us—because the bottom line is, it's our money.

The biggest revenue generator in Canada, by far, is our personal income tax. And because you can't draw water from an empty well, the government squeezes as much as it can from the most bountiful sources: people who are wealthy. Our progressive tax system is designed to impose a much higher tax rate on the rich than on the poor. The more you earn, the higher percentage of your income you are compelled to pay.

Accordingly, 55.9 percent of the nation's personal tax revenue in 2017 came from the top 20 percent of Canadian earners, and 14.7 percent of total tax revenue came from the top 1 percent.[2]

That's a ton—but it reflects the income inequality in our country, and it's why so many of us say it's right and fair that the rich should pay more. It's their "fair share."

---

[2] Charles Lammam, Hugh MacIntyre, and Milagros Palacios, "Measuring the Distribution of Taxes in Canada: Do the Rich Pay Their 'Fair Share'?" *Towards a Better Understanding of Income Inequality in Canada,* Fraser Institute, (November 30, 2017): 186–198, https://www.fraserinstitute.org/sites/default/files/measuring-the-distribution-of-taxes-in-canada.pdf.

But it's a little more complicated than that. When we recite the mantra that the rich should pay more, we tend to ignore other ways they contribute to our social well-being. We neglect how many jobs they create. We're blind to how their success benefits the economy.

Take Jeff Bezos, for example. He was the richest man in the world, worth $131 billion before his divorce—but he was no thief. He didn't take other people's hard-earned money and stash it all in his pocket. Bezos started selling books out of his garage and turned his business into Amazon, the world's largest retailer—and the world's largest job creator. In 2018, Amazon had more than 647,000 employees, and all of them—not just Bezos—paid taxes.

That's the sort of contribution the wealthy can make. It's much more than their personal tax payments. And this isn't true only for the super wealthy. It's true for anyone who starts a business.

My partners and I created a business that now employs about sixty people. Their jobs wouldn't be there if we hadn't taken a risk, invested our money, and worked our butts off to build a successful practice. Our employees are talented and hardworking, and I don't doubt for a minute that they'd have jobs somewhere else if they didn't work for us—but there'd still be sixty fewer jobs available on the market.

That's the spillover effect of entrepreneurship. Business owners are the sources of the income their employees declare and pay taxes on.

I'm not advocating that our wealthiest earners shouldn't pay more than a blue-collar worker who can barely afford to keep his family sheltered and fed. Far from it. I feel very strongly that, under our existing standards, the wealthy should pay a much higher tax rate than those at the bottom. But just how much higher?

That's the question we all have to ask, because—remember the Laffer Curve? When you tax too much, you reach a point where returns start to fall. And I think we're at or already past that point. In my opinion, which I've formed after years of experience working with top earners, the peak resides somewhere around the 50 percent mark. That's the tipping point on the Laffer Curve.

When the government takes more than that, it ends up raising a lot less revenue because that's when the wealthy start to change their behavior. They begin to seek ways to aggressively avoid paying what they owe. We've already seen it happen here in Canada. As stated earlier, in 2015, the government imposed a 4 percent increase in the tax rate for people who made more than $200,000. And it projected that the measure would bring in an additional $3.2 billion in revenue.

Only it didn't. The next year, the government collected $4.6 billion less that what it had budgeted for, because people in its targeted tax bracket—the top earners in Canada—changed their behavior and took measures to avoid paying what they were expected to. That's how the Laffer Curve works. Once you hit the top of the curve, everything goes downhill.

And now look at where we are today: In 2019, the tax rate in Canada for income over roughly $210,000 was 33 percent—and that was just the federal income tax. In Newfoundland and Labrador, people who earned more than $188,000 paid an additional 18.3 percent. Nova Scotians who made more than $150,000 paid an additional 21 percent. In New Brunswick, the top tax tier paid an additional 20.3 percent. In Ontario and Quebec, people pay a 54 percent combined income tax on everything they earn in excess of about $200,000. And some federal parties want to raise that highest income tax bracket by an additional 2 percent.

That means the people in the highest tax bracket in those provinces are paying more than half their income in taxes. That's reckless, in my view, because it's on the downhill slope of the Laffer Curve. It's also shameful because it prevents us from attracting the most desirable workers—especially when our nearest neighbor, the United States, has much more favorable rates. In states like Texas, Washington, and Florida, where they have no state personal income tax, the highest tax rate is 37 percent.

I brought this up during a presentation I made before the House of Commons Finance Committee about the 2019 federal budget. I pointed out that a player for the Toronto Maple Leafs would pay 54 percent of his salary in income taxes—considerably more than he'd have to pay if he played in Dallas or Tampa Bay or Seattle. This wasn't just an idea I made up to get my point across. It has actually happened.

Steven Stamkos, the captain of the National Hockey League's Tampa Bay Lightning—and a six-time NHL All-Star—was born and raised in Markham, Ontario. He's represented Canada in the World Junior Ice Hockey Championships, the

Men's World Championship, the Winter Olympics, the World Championships, and the FIH Hockey World Cup.

He's a Canadian through and through, but in 2016, when he could have chosen to become a free agent, he signed an eight-year contract to remain in Tampa. Stamkos gets paid $8.5 million per year, which would put him in the top tax bracket anywhere. But Florida has no state income tax, so the most he has to pay is the American federal income tax of 37 percent.

If Stamkos played for the Toronto Maple Leafs and was a Canadian resident for income tax purposes, his federal and Ontario income tax would amount to about 54 percent—17 percent more than he has to pay in Florida. Even if he'd become a free agent and signed for more money to play in Toronto, he'd likely have wound up taking home less than he does in Florida. Cross-border professional-athlete taxation is a lot more complex than I'm describing here, but you get my point.

This wouldn't be so disconcerting if it were just one or two hockey players, but in the more than twenty-five years that I've been in practice, I have never seen so many wealthy individuals leave Canada or change their legal residency to another country just so they could reduce their tax obligations. I probably have five times as many clients becoming nonresidents now as I've had at any time in my career.

Everyone should pay his fair share. That's a simple, declarative statement, and I happen to agree with it. But how much is fair? That's what we can't seem to agree upon. For a lot of Canadians, "fair share" has become a rallying cry for squeezing more and

KIM G C MOODY

more money out of the wealthy—based solely on their wealth and regardless of the contributions they make to our society beyond their tax obligations.

"Fair share," for those Canadians, is just a demand that the rich pay more—much more. I have no doubt that if our government created a 90 percent tax bracket for the wealthy, the Left would still say it's not enough, that the rich still aren't paying their "fair share." I can't even imagine what they think the wealthy's "fair share" should be. But to me, it's whatever the law says it is.

My job as a tax accountant is to make sure that people pay what they legally owe—no more and no less. If the wealthy are filing their tax returns, and they're complying with the law, then I'd say they're paying their fair share—because that's what our legislators decided they should pay. If our legislators think the top rate is unfair, and they increase it to make the wealthy pay their "fair share," then I'll say the new rate they come up with is fair. No matter what it is, no matter what its long-term effect might be, we'll have to live with it.

As far as I'm concerned, while anything above 50 percent may be the wealthy's "fair share"—it's most certainly on the wrong side of the Laffer Curve. So, watch out what you wish for, because you just might get it. The bottom line is that if you tax the wealthy at a rate higher than 50 percent, you risk damaging the economy—and there's nothing fair about that. The wealthy are already paying an awful lot, and I don't know that they'll accept paying more.

During and after his 2015 campaign, Prime Minister Trudeau kept saying that the wealthy needed to pay their "fair share." This alienated wealth creators, because that term has become a shibboleth for class warriors who are promoting identity politics that cause more harm than good. They're pitting the wealthy against the poor, the white against the nonwhite, male against female, young against old—and I'm really not sure why, because I believe none of that is helpful to our society.

There's no doubt that we have societal issues that need to be addressed and corrected. Certainly, the gap between the rich and the poor is growing ever wider. But I think fomenting discontent just makes things worse because you can't solve income inequality with a stroke of a prime minister's pen. Even if you could, the added money you'd be taking from the wealthy would go to the government. You'd be trusting politicians and bureaucrats to distribute it in the right manner—and our record isn't very good in that area.

It also wouldn't address the question of whether increasing taxes is the right and only way to deal with poverty and income inequality—because if you raise taxes to the point that the wealthy move their businesses or wealth out of the country, then what good have you done? And don't think for a minute that it won't happen—because it's happening now. The wealthy are increasingly deploying their investment capital to places other than Canada—especially to the United States, where President Donald Trump's tax reforms have created a fertile garden for foreign investments to grow.

Just ten years ago, at the height of the Great Recession, the effects of the financial crisis weren't as great in Alberta as they were in most of North America, thanks to a robust oil and gas industry that was expanding, rather than contracting, in the province. But after 2015, because of a variety of policies that have hurt the oil and gas industry (including the restriction of building pipeline access), we're in a very depressed situation, with very low foreign capital investment. Money isn't flowing in anymore. It's flowing out.

I said earlier that wealthy individuals are leaving Canada at a greater rate than I've ever seen before—but what's even more remarkable is how much private investment capital is being deployed into the US. The overall business environment south of the border, combined with a much friendlier tax environment there, is sucking business away from Canada at a higher rate than I've ever seen. And that scares me because if we can't stop it, we're going to see a lot of Canadian jobs shift south too.

Nothing good happens when we raise our job creators' taxes to an intolerable level. Going down that road is just crazy. And what's really sad is that it's unnecessary too—because there is a way to increase taxes on the wealthy and have them agree, with no reservations, that they're paying their fair share. As stated earlier in this book, it's the consumption tax.

———————•——————

I am convinced that the best way to ensure that everyone pays his fair share of taxes is to eliminate or at least dramatically reduce taxation of income, and to replace it with a tax on spending.

I'm optimistic it will work—and it's time people understood how and why. Here's how: A consumption tax—also known as a value-added tax—is like a sales tax on steroids. The government determines how much to tax all expenses, and everybody, the wealthy *and* the poor, pays the same percentage.

If the government sets the consumption tax at 33 percent and you want to download that new Taylor Swift album for $18, it'll cost you $24. If you decide to buy a new car for $30,000, you'll pay $40,000. If you decide to buy a yacht for $3 million, you'll pay $4 million. No matter what you spend your money on, you'll pay an additional 33 percent of what it costs to the government.

Does that sound insane? If it does, I think you've forgotten that a consumption tax wouldn't be in addition to the income tax—it would replace it. And this would be a good thing, because income tax is basically retrogressive since it's *not* a wealth tax.

The poor have to pay income taxes if they have a certain level of income, and they wind up paying a larger share of what they own than wealthy people, who are likewise taxed only on their income—not their wealth. We don't take away the money they already have, just a percentage of the new money they earn.

A consumption tax is fairer because everyone, rich or poor, gets to keep every dollar they earn and pay tax only on what they spend. As an added bonus, they'll never again worry about getting their tax return in by the April 30 deadline, because tax returns will vanish. When nobody's taxing your income, there's no need to report it.

I've heard people say that a consumption tax is unfair, because the poor and the wealthy pay the same amount in taxes when they buy the same items. And it's true—they'll pay the same tax when they buy a smartphone or a book or a bottle of whiskey. But only when they buy the exact same thing. They'll pay identical taxes only when they buy identical items. And, let's face it, that's just not going to happen.

Do you think a billionaire is going to buy the same car as someone who makes $50,000 a year? How many billionaires have you seen tooling around town in a used Corolla? That billionaire is more likely to be found driving a Maserati. And he very well may have a Ferrari and a Lamborghini and a Rolls collecting dust in his garage.

When he goes on vacation, he's probably not renting a motel room on the Jersey Shore and eating fast food for a week alongside one of his lower-salaried employees. He's much more likely to be flying first class to the Seychelles or Bali and spending a week or two at a five-star resort.

They're both paying consumption tax, and it's the same percentage of what they're spending—but the billionaire boss is spending much more than his employee. That means he's forking over a lot more in consumption tax too. He's buying more expensive stuff, so he's paying a much larger consumption tax.

Replacing the income tax with a consumption tax would ensure that everyone in Canada pays his fair share, though I doubt such a radical change could ever make it through Parliament. The idea is essentially a nonstarter.

But I think the idea should be taught in colleges and universities—if for no other reason than that's what higher learning is supposed to encompass: the exchange of ideas.

Sadly, however, there aren't many institutions in our country that teach core entrepreneurial skills. They teach economics, and they offer accounting courses, but where are the core courses that teach our kids how to take risks and how to be successful in business? There aren't any. Not at the university level.

When I started my business, I didn't have a clue what to do or where to begin. University didn't prepare me even a little bit.

I was lucky though. I came from a family of entrepreneurs who made it very clear to me that I needed to deploy my capital very diligently and that I would have to take some risks. They had to be *smart* risks, so I had to do market research to ensure that there actually was a market out there for me.

I had to ask, what was my opportunity? How would I do it better? What made me uniquely positioned to be successful? These are the things they don't teach in college, because striving to succeed conflicts with the lofty notion that everyone should be equal in every way. But that's just not how the world works. The world has always had people who have an idea and patiently develop a plan to bring it to fruition. They have what it takes to deploy their strategy thoughtfully, methodically, and with careful risk assessments—the exact things academics can't teach, because they can't even imagine them. But these core principles need to be integrated into the business and economics courses on our campuses.

Entrepreneurs build businesses that didn't exist before they hatched the ideas that created them. They create a need for new products, they open up new chains of supply and demand, and they put people to work. When they do that well enough to become wealthy, we should not demonize them. We should encourage more people to do what they did, to study their success and try to build something even better.

———•———•———•———

Young people need to be told that BOMAD—the Bank of Mom and Dad—won't be around forever, and that they need to learn the benefits of hard work, careful deployment of capital, and the value of taking calculated risks so they can deploy them and be successful on their own. And they need to be taught that there are almost always two or more sides to every story, that the prevailing ideology they may hear in high school and university is not the only one out there, and that they should always keep an open mind to the alternatives.

Maybe we don't want a consumption tax. Maybe it's a terrible idea. But at the very least, we should be open to discussing it.

CHAPTER 9

Is It Fake News?

J ust before I began writing this book, an article in one of Canada's most-read newspapers caught my eye. The story—written by the paper's top financial reporter—addressed the fallout from the 2016 income tax hike, and it zeroed in on the "fact" that wealthy Canadians didn't leave the country when the increases went into effect—despite predictions and my experience to the contrary. To support her "reporting," the writer cited statistics provided by Canada's parliamentary budget officer.

I read that story, and my first impression was that it was a great big bundle of nonsense. So I decided to waste a little time digging into the budget officer's report, just to confirm that I was right. The report was about twenty-five pages long, and it was pretty easy to read—and as I suspected, it said nothing about the rich leaving Canada. Not a word. It didn't even offer a comment on the tax increase's impact on wealthy citizens.

But it did say that if the government hadn't increased the tax rate on people with higher incomes, it would have collected $3.6 billion *more* in tax revenues in that one year alone.

The report was a textbook example of how the Laffer Curve applies to taxation, and it was practically leaping off the page. But you wouldn't have known that if you'd read the newspaper article because the paper's "financial reporter" failed to report it. Maybe she didn't fully grasp its significance. Or maybe she missed the point because it didn't conform to her expectations.

Or maybe it was both. It struck me that the writer had started out with a conclusion in mind and proceeded to search only for "facts" that supported it. There was a much more important story to be told in the budget officer's report, but it didn't fit her agenda—so she chose not to tell it.

I believe that reporter wrote the story to trumpet the ideology of her employer, a major newspaper that consistently delivers articles about income inequality and how the rich need to be taxed more. She got the story wrong—but that's okay. It delivered the message the editors wanted. That's just how things seem to work these days.

But I wonder, does the average reader know that? I don't think so. I think the average person reads the article, doesn't understand the complexity of the issue, and doesn't consider spending the time and effort needed to do some research and dig out the truth.

My guess is that the average reader just accepts the headline and the story at face value. "It's in the newspaper, so it must be right. And, besides, who cares? I agree with it." That's what the average reader thinks. As for me, I think that's dangerous.

Here's an undeniable truth: If you have an income, you pay taxes. Whether you're a multibillionaire business owner with a fleet of private jets, a star athlete with an eight-figure salary, or a blue-collar worker living paycheck to paycheck . . . if you make money, you pay taxes.

Income tax is the government's largest source of revenue, and it's one of the biggest—if not *the* biggest—expenditures each of us makes individually. Taxes are our investment in our country and in our community, so we really should care about how our government decides the amount we must pay and what it does with the money we pay out.

All that information is readily available—but you'll be hard-pressed to find it in most of our newspapers and magazines. Instead of facts, too often these days the media gives us their ideological message—a smidgen of facts with a heaping dose of spin that they deliver over and over again: "The rich aren't paying their fair share." "Sure," they say, "wealthy people already pay more. But they don't pay nearly enough. They should pay much, much more. And even more than that."

When I was growing up, I just assumed that journalists told the truth. I assumed that their reporting was always objective, and that facts were, well—facts. What I didn't understand was how easy it was to frame public opinion by selectively presenting the facts they liked and withholding the ones they didn't.

I was naïve then, but I'm more experienced now. I've learned that our news media is quite adept at cherry-picking facts to support their ideological message. They do it all the time—especially when it comes to reporting news about taxes and politics. Those areas are inherently intertwined, and I know

now that the "facts" we see in the print media often reflect the ideologies of the people who publish them.

I've witnessed this throughout my career, but never so much as I have in the past four or five years. More and more, I'm seeing the media slant their reports to sway opinion—and that is alarming.

———————•———————

For nerds like me, there's no shortage of articles in the academic literature that present the facts about taxes. But it does appear to me that often the mainstream media doesn't seem to care about objective reporting anymore—especially when it comes to the economy and taxes. They start out by deciding what they want to say, and then they tailor the facts to suit their message.

In many cases, their articles are just flat-out wrong. Maybe they haven't done their homework, or maybe they don't understand the material. It doesn't really matter though, because they'll write their story anyway.

It's not a problem if what they write has no basis in fact because they're not really here to report the facts; they're here to sell newspapers and advertising. Their goal is to keep the customer satisfied. If it conforms with management's ideology—and if it's what their readers want to read—then it's good to go. Roll the presses.

That's just how it is, but I can't understand how anyone can be happy about that. As far as I'm concerned, ideology belongs in opinion columns—not in objective reporting. Most readers don't know the fine details and nuances of taxes, and publishing misinformation and putting ideology ahead of facts just makes them less informed.

Maybe I'm old-fashioned, but I believe the truth matters. In this "enlightened" age of fake news and audience algorithms, I'm feeling more and more like I'm in the minority.

But why would anyone want to publish half-truths and lies? Who benefits from publishing falsehoods about the tax statutes or policy? Who wins, and why?

When you tailor the "facts" to advance your ideology, there's a good chance you'll succeed in persuading a large number of your readers to support a political party that subscribes to your point of view. If you're on the left—and a large number of Canadian newspapers and magazines are—and you spread so-called factual messages about how the rich don't pay their fair share, you'll ultimately get what you want: a government that's determined to tax the rich, even if it ultimately hurts everyone.

Quality newspapers used to maintain a rock-solid wall between their newsrooms and their editorial pages. The newsrooms reported the news—the fact-based stories that kept the readers informed—and the editorial pages presented opinions and commentary that most often reflected the views of the publisher.

But today, that wall is made of sand. Newspapers are struggling everywhere, thanks to the internet, Google's and Facebook's domination of advertising revenue, and twenty-four-hour cable news networks. Traditional newspaper advertising—especially classified advertising—has practically vanished, and newspapers are either drastically cutting staff or going out of business entirely. In a desperate effort to survive, many of them have abandoned their mission to present the facts.

Instead, they've decided to become framers of public opinion on both sides of their crumbled wall, whether it's in the news section or the op-ed pages. Controversy, anger, and extreme views—that's what sells newspapers, and selling newspapers is all that matters. Reporting is out. Advocacy is in.

For some newspapers, it's the key to survival. But for reporters who don't subscribe to this new reality, it's the writing on their tombstone. On the one hand, we're witnessing evolution—the survival of the fittest. But on the other hand, we're seeing the demise of professional standards in a centuries-old news delivery system and the widespread elimination of thousands of jobs and business opportunities the industry used to support.

Nobody is happy about any of this, which is why the Trudeau government recently passed legislation to inject $600 million into the national budget to support a dying business. The government has created a new classification—"registered journalist organizations"—that it will treat in much the same way it registers charities. If a registered journalist organization meets certain conditions, it will be eligible to issue charitable tax receipts to anyone who donates to it.

The government also is proposing to offer 25 percent refundable tax incentives for hiring journalists, up to a maximum salary of approximately $55,000. If a newspaper hires a reporter and pays her $55,000, the government will give the journalist organization a refund check of just below $14,000.

And finally, the government would like to offer personal tax credits to anyone who subscribes to the journalist organizations' publications—up to a subscription price of $500.

These measures might save a subset of some newspapers, but let's step back and think about all of this for a minute, because $600 million is an awful lot of money to keep a dying industry on a respirator. Nobody wants to see newspapers die, but is it the government's job to keep them alive? What other failing industries should Ottawa support? Blacksmiths? Horse-drawn-carriage makers? Landline phone manufacturers?

And is providing "tax incentives" the appropriate policy response? Shouldn't we be looking at the core reasons why newspapers are struggling? It seems to me that the digital technology giants like Google and Facebook are the key culprits here. They seem to be dominating advertising revenue while paying nothing for content. Are there any solutions? I'm not sure.

Also, think about the pressure this legislation puts on the publishers. If they face going out of business without a slice of that $600 million pie, it stands to reason that they'll do everything they can to butter the bread of everyone involved in giving them a grant.

Do you think that might affect how they cover the news? Do you think they'll feel comfortable delivering factual, unbiased reports that are critical of the government when their future is on the line? Even if they can maintain their objectivity, do you think they'll be able to persuade their readers that, in fact, they're doing just that? If the government is supporting them, isn't every word they write suspect?

I think this puts all of us right on the edge of a cliff, a slippery slope that handcuffs the press instead of freeing it. I expect this plan will encourage cheerleading for the government, a fear of biting the hand that feeds us. And I think that risks creating a very serious threat to our democracy—because if you subsidize one-sided, pro-government reporting, you can be sure you'll get more of it.

If you want to install a socialist regime in Canada, just connect the dots. Step one: control the media. Step two: tax the rich. Step three: put on your rose-colored glasses. We're on our way.

———•———

The Canadian economy right now is like a leaky boat foundering in choppy seas, and the measures it takes to stay afloat and sail on to clear waters should concern all of us. We're making critical decisions about taxes, about nationalizing industries, about rules and regulations, about imports and exports. Our decisions will affect all of us, so we should insist that our mainstream media deliver timely, accurate, and balanced reporting to keep us informed.

In the US, President Trump's tax cuts have contributed to a significant uptick in the US economy. Jobs are plentiful, and the unemployment rate is the lowest it's been in half a century.

And what is Canada doing to compete? Nothing. Ottawa appears to be comfortable holding its cards while it's being undercut by our neighbors to the south. Reduce tax rates? "Nah, we'll be fine." Fight the gorilla? "Nah, it's too hard."

We've made no effort to respond to their corporate tax rate reduction. We're not responding to their repatriation of money. US companies are aggressively writing off their business assets, and we show no inclination to let Canadian companies do the same.

Compete? "Nah, maybe next time." We're doing nothing. We've chosen inaction—and worst of all, we're not even having a healthy discussion of whether or not that's our best response. Instead, I see ideologues in our left-leaning newspapers saying we should not respond to US competitiveness. And, regrettably, I see very few opinions to the contrary.

Our media is framing popular opinion by tamping down alternative thinking, and that should be triggering alarms all around us. We should all be asking, "How do we figure out what's false or misleading? How do we separate that from what's true and accurate—especially when it concerns our taxes and our economy? And if we can't get the facts from our main-stream media, where *can* we get them?"

Sadly, it's not as easy to find them as it used to be. But it's not impossible. We need to read with a critical eye, and we need to select and follow writers we trust, whether they are news reporters or opinion writers. We need to vet them, just as we would vet a job candidate. We need to feel comfortable that they're telling us the unvarnished truth, whether we like it or not. And we need to feel comfortable with alternative points of view that are thoughtful and not politicized.

In my field, taxes, I know I can trust material put out by the Canadian Tax Foundation, an organization of academics, prac-titioners, and government bureaucrats who produce top-quality and, for the most part, neutral writing. The CTF's offerings include some ideological thinking, but generally everything is well researched.

I read everything written by Jack Mintz, one of Canada's leading economists. As for our national and community newspapers, I've come to the conclusion that they're all suspect, no matter whether they lean left or right (though most tilt heavily to the left).

They're not reporting fake news . . . but they're not reporting real news either. They're reporting spin—bent facts and selective truths whose presentation is intentionally misleading, stories designed not to inform readers, but to affirm the writers' ideologies.

I believe in democracy, and I believe most of my fellow Canadians do too. I believe in a government of leaders who represent all of us and work tirelessly to make our lives better. And I cherish the notion that we get to choose those leaders—a privilege that comes with a responsibility to keep those same people in check. But to do that well, we need to be well informed. We need to be armed with raw facts, not facts that have been rinsed, spun, and hung out to dry.

My specialty is taxes, and I can say with full confidence that our media is letting us down. When the facts don't fit their ideology, they'll ignore them or bend them to make them work. And that's dangerous, because taxes matter. They affect everything we do, every day of our lives. We need to be informed, and we deserve—we should *demand*—that our media gives us an honest account of the news.

CHAPTER 10

So How, Exactly, Should We Tax?

doubt there's a place in the free world where people don't complain about the government. It takes away our hard-earned money and imposes countless rules and regulations that stop us from doing whatever we want, whenever we want.

But we need government, because the alternative is much worse.

The alternative is anarchy. And that is not an option.

The choice is clear, but it comes with some personal responsibilities. If you want to live in a governed society, you must provide the government with a steady stream of revenue—because governments don't work for free. They can't exist without money.

We can't support a military, police departments, justice system, public educational institutions, highways and roads, and health services without public funding. Without a source of income, a government can't sustain its functions.

We can debate around the clock how much money our government should take from us. Those of us who lean left generally say it should take more so it can provide us with more services than it already does. Those of us who lean right say government should be less involved in our day-to-day affairs, and that it should take less.

I believe, at a base level, that our federal, provincial, and local governments should provide services that benefit all of us and that they should take care of people who are unable to take care of all their needs themselves.

Our government should provide basic medical care. It should maintain our highways. It should provide educational services, law enforcement, and a judicial system. It should maintain a military and supply it with the weapons it needs to protect us. But it can't do any of these things if it doesn't have money to pay for them.

That's what taxes are for. As much as we hate them, we simply can't live without them. So there really should be no debating whether or not to tax. The only thing worth debating is how.

For more than a century, income taxes have been the largest source of revenue in Canada. I think the time has come to reconsider that.

Taxing income is not the only way our government can collect the revenue it needs to provide services and sustain itself. There are many other methods that, at the very least, are worth discussing.

One is a wealth tax: taxing people not on how much they earn, but on how much they own.

Consider this: when you tax income, a retired multibillionaire who now makes $40,000 a year and a single mom of two young kids who makes $40,000 a year have the same taxable income.

He owns a few mansions and a private island in the Pacific. She rents a one-bedroom apartment and rides two buses to get to work. But their income is the same, so they're taxed the same amount.

But a wealth tax treats them differently. It taxes their bank accounts, the value of their investments, and their tangible possessions. His wealth is in the billions; hers is practically nonexistent. And they're taxed accordingly.

To some people, that sounds fair. To others, it sounds like punishment for being rich. But whether it's fair or foul, exactly how do you compute wealth?

Who decides what that billionaire's mansions are worth?

If he buys a $250,000 car and wrecks it, what's it worth? If he invests a few million bucks in a start-up that could make billions—or go broke in six months—what's it worth? If he puts all his money in the stock market, which can fluctuate dramatically every half hour, when and how do you decide what his portfolio is worth?

The variables, fluctuations, and subjective decisions inherent in taxing wealth don't occur when you tax income. Whether you're a billionaire or a schoolteacher, your income is a quantifiable amount that isn't subject to as much interpretation. It's how much money you make, plain and simple. It's why taxing income is much easier than taxing wealth.

Another potential source of revenue is a "sin tax"—a surcharge on items that give us sensory pleasure, such as alcohol and tobacco, . . . and even sugary sodas and junk food. The revenue from sin taxes is theoretically used to combat alcoholism, tobacco addiction, and obesity.

And finally, there's a consumption tax. In most of the country, we already have one in the form of sales tax. But we're not doing it right, and we're not doing it enough.

————•————

Let's make one thing clear: I am not an economist. I recognize and acknowledge that there are people who are better educated and more qualified than I am to discuss economic theory and taxation policy.

But I've been a tax consultant for decades, and I think my practical experience in the field should, at the very least, be considered. I think I deserve to be heard because my experience has led me to conclude that there's likely a better way, and that the time is long past due to convene a commission to consider all our options and make some dramatic changes.

We need to sit down, look at our chief source of revenues, and ask ourselves, "What is the goal of our income tax? Is it simply to raise money? Is it policy-oriented? Is it for income redistribution? Where is it now, where is it heading, and what should it look like for the wealthy, the so-called middle class, the working class, and the poor?"

And when we ask these questions, we have to stop pretending that wealth redistribution is not part of the package. Some of our politicians hate the term *wealth distribution*, but it's exactly what we're accomplishing today. We have a progressive tax system—meaning, people with higher incomes pay higher tax rates, and the government uses their money to provide social programs that are designed to help the poor.

If that isn't wealth distribution, then the term has no meaning whatsoever. So let's just call it what it is. But let's stop demonizing it too—because there's nothing wrong with redistributing wealth to serve the common good.

Too often, though, our government isn't fully transparent about what it does with our taxes. Take, for example, the introduction of a carbon tax. Several provinces have introduced a carbon tax as a way to cut emissions that contribute to climate change. If you live in a province that has the tax, you pay it every time you fill up your gas tank and every time you pay your electric and heating bill.

And that's fine. If you believe a carbon tax will lower emissions, then it's a sensible way to fight climate change.

But if that's the reason for imposing a carbon tax, why would you offer refunds and rebates to people whose income is below a certain threshold? Or to large-emitter companies? You can't save the earth if you're handing out exemptions to some people. That's like giving them a license to keep on destroying it. Are the poor, unlike the wealthy, entitled to pollute?

I think the carbon tax should land squarely in the sin tax category. We impose high taxes on tobacco products and alcohol in the hopes that people who buy them will reconsider their smoking and drinking habits. It's essentially a regressive tax because the wealthy and the poor pay the same amount per pack of cigarettes or bottle of whiskey. It's intended to achieve a desired goal—and it often works.

Why should a carbon tax be any different? If the idea is to get people to stop buying gas-guzzling SUVs, to turn off the lights, to lower the thermostat in the winter and raise it in the summer—then we're not going to change people's behavior by offering them rebates when their income is low.

That rebate is a form of wealth redistribution—but it isn't a good one. Offering rebates on carbon taxes essentially says we're trying to save the world, but not everyone has to join the effort. I think that's a terrible way to levy taxes.

———————

Canada started taxing income in 1917 as a temporary measure to fund the country's involvement in World War I.

A century later, that "temporary" income tax is still with us.

Should it be though? Should we still be depending on taxpayers' income to provide revenue for our government?

I think we should be. I think the income tax should have a place in our tax statute, but not at its current level. It should continue to be part of an overall taxation package, but it shouldn't be the largest part anymore.

I am convinced that a consumption tax—also called a Value-Added Tax (VAT)—should play a much more prominent role than it does today.

In all Canadian provinces except Alberta, Northwest Territories, Nunavut, and Yukon, people pay a Harmonized Sales Tax (HST) on all purchases, with the exception of basic food items and some other exemptions. The HST is the sum of the 5 percent federal Goods and Services Tax (GST) and the Provincial Sales Tax (PST), which varies from province to province, but is generally somewhere between 8 and 10 percent.

I think the HST should be higher than that—much higher, in fact—so long as it's designed to avoid hurting the poor.

I believe a consumption tax that exempts expenses for basic necessities like groceries, health care, and education will provide a much more sensible—and potentially more lucrative—way of raising revenue than the income tax.

I say that because the income tax has peaked and is tipping over to the wrong side of the Laffer Curve. If we keep increasing personal income tax rates on the wealthy, we'll discourage entrepreneurship and the incentive to earn more money.

Increasing the consumption tax, on the other hand, will tax the wealthy not on how much they earn, but on how much they spend.

It's true that if they choose to live frugally—if they'd rather buy a used Volkswagen than a shiny new Mercedes—they'll save more of their money. A consumption tax gives them that choice.

But I haven't met very many wealthy people who choose to live the life of the poor. Wealthy people tend to spend top dollar for their possessions, and I don't believe that raising the tax rate on what they spend will persuade them to change their lifestyle.

———————•———————

It's obvious to me that the time has come—in fact, it came many years ago—to convene a commission to reexamine every aspect of Canada's tax policy. We need to take a hard look at how much revenue we need to provide essential government services and how best to collect it.

That's what we *should* do. But will we? I doubt it. I think politics will, unfortunately, get in the way.

In the past, our government has zigzagged between left and right of center, without veering very far to either side. But in the last four years, we've been skating further and further to the left—much further than I've ever seen. And with the 2019 federal election now over and the Liberal party winning a minority government (likely to be supported by the left-leaning NDP), it is likely Canada will be staying left for a while.

We are attacking some of the core principles of capitalism. We've imposed very high income tax rates on individuals and corporations that are drastically curtailing entrepreneurship and making it increasingly harder to compete with the gorilla south of our border—the US.

If we continue down the path of higher taxes, and if we persist in attacking our job creators, I worry about what will happen to us in the not-too-distant future. I think our country will suffer greatly if we stay on this path.

But why are we even on this path? Why are we attacking entrepreneurial spirit?

I think it's because of ignorance. I'm shocked at what our kids are being taught about how an economy works, how jobs are created, and how wealth is accumulated. From secondary school right through university, they're being taught only one side of the story.

And it isn't just in school. They're getting it from the media too.

Social media has amplified a "Hollywood effect," where our kids' heroes are rock stars and movie stars who keep their perfect lives on constant display on Facebook, Instagram, and Twitter.

They are rich, they are famous, and they're going to change the world. They'll lead, and our kids will follow.

We've all read stories about celebrities who hopscotch across the globe to meet with world leaders and press for measures to combat the effects of climate change. The audience just eats that up—but why don't they notice that so many of those movie stars and entertainers live in large-footprint mansions and are traveling from conference to conference in fuel-guzzling private planes?

To me, the hypocrisy of all that is just astonishing. But the Hollywood effect is very powerful. The stars are influential not only with the public—but with politicians too. And for the most part, they lean far to the left. They make it difficult for people who hold conservative views to get equal time. It's very hard to compete with star power. All we can do is try.

A few months before I wrote this book, I was invited to comment on television about some changes the government made to the Income Tax Act. I sent a clip of the show to my family after my appearance, and my son, who was in the eleventh grade, showed it to his social studies teacher.

The teacher liked what he saw, and he invited me to come speak to his twelfth-grade social studies students—about two hundred kids in all. I accepted, and I made plans to deliver an hour-and-a-half-long lecture on basic tax and economic policy.

I arrived at the school concerned that the kids would have already made up their minds on the issues I wanted to discuss.

But to my surprise, a lot of those kids asked some very interesting questions.

I walked in assuming that they wouldn't be able to see both sides of the issue, and I walked away thinking that the opposite was true. Those kids changed my mind. They were eager to hear some intelligent and logical points of view that challenged the party line.

I felt excited when I left. And I was thrilled, just two days later, when I received an email from a father who had been at my lecture.

He said he wanted to thank me. He said he'd seen me lecture elsewhere, and that he'd always liked what I had to say, and he was delighted that his son came home feeling very encouraged about my lecture.

I had gotten through to someone. That was satisfying. And it gave me hope.

Canada's Income Tax Act is overwrought, overcomplicated, over-*everything*. It's a behemoth that needs to be tamed. And it *can* be tamed—if our political leaders can be persuaded to take on the hard job of dealing with it.

It's been more than half a century since we had a comprehensive review of our country's tax statute. The Royal Commission on Taxation spent four years studying the tax system before it issued its report in 1966, and we waited six more years for major tax reform to come into effect in 1972.

More than fifty years on, it's time to do it again. Our Income Tax Act has become as thick as sludge, a system so complex that even average taxpayers need people like me to help them figure out just how much they have to pay.

It needs an overhaul, with an eye on simplicity.

Tax is one of the most complex topics in the universe, and I don't think we'll ever succeed in reforming things to the point that we can fill out our returns on postcards. But I do think we can make everything easier to understand and administer. The average Canadian really shouldn't have to hire an accountant or a tax service to figure out how much he owes the government.

Filling out a tax return has become horribly complex and absurdly time-consuming. What's worse is that even when we spend countless hours trying to get it right, it's almost guaranteed that we won't.

We need a government. But we need one that serves people. So long as we continue to tolerate a tax system that is incomprehensible to most Canadians, we're doing ourselves a great disservice.

The time has come to tear the tax statutes apart and rebuild them from scratch.

It will be the biggest favor we can do for ourselves.

CHAPTER 11

Should We Continue the Conversation?

Make no mistake: the time has come to blow up our arcane and nonproductive Income Tax Act. We need to rewrite it from top to bottom.

Make no mistake about this too: it won't happen anytime soon. Nobody's going to grab the bull by the horns and bring it to submission because it's a monumental task, and we don't take those on anymore.

Sure, it's broken, but that doesn't mean we're going to fix it. And let's be clear: a piecemeal approach to fixing something is not the answer—despite those who say we can deal with the problems in our tax system with targeted solutions.

Fixing problems is hard—much harder than just kicking them down the road. So, for the foreseeable future, we'll keep playing the hand we've been dealt. The tax statute we have will be the tax statute we get.

And the truth is, I can deal with that. Standing pat won't hurt me, because when people can't make heads or tails of the tax laws, I'm one of the people they come to.

I've been in the tax business for more than twenty-five years, and I know how to find answers to very difficult questions. It's the one thing I'm really good at.

Ask anyone who knows me, and they'll tell you I carry the Income Tax Act everywhere—on dates with my wife, to dinner, to the theater, to hockey games, to bed. Where accountants gather, I'm the life of the "tax party."

But put me on a soapbox, and here's what I'll tell you:

- Our taxes have a greater material impact on our overall net worth and on our ability to retire and save than just about anything else we encounter in our lives. The tax statutes are very hard to read—most people can't bear to even glance at them—but we ignore them at our own peril. We need to be well educated about taxes because the price of ignorance is just too high.

- Far too many people call themselves tax experts, but far too many of them aren't. It's easy to say; it's hard to prove. We need to scrutinize anyone who purports to be highly knowledgeable about taxes, because if we don't, the results can be catastrophic. We need to ask: What are your credentials? How experienced are you? Who are your clients? What can you accomplish?

- We need to learn and understand the importance of good tax policy because we should never blindly believe what our politicians tell us. We need to dig down deep into the details because policies matter.

———————

Tax is a hard subject, but it's important. It determines our future.

I'm passionate about it because I'm a tax consultant. I help my clients navigate the tax statutes. I make sure they pay the government exactly what they owe—nothing more (which is wasteful) and nothing less (which is risky).

It's what I do. It's my job. And because I insist on doing it well, I stay actively involved in the tax community, which helps me better understand the tax statutes and enables me to be an influential voice in my colleagues' efforts to make positive changes.

My firm, Moodys Tax—a combination of Moodys Tax Law LLP (a tax law firm) and Moodys Private Client LLP (an accounting firm)—comprises a team of Canadian and US lawyers and accountants who understand that everyone's tax situation is unique. We combine our talent, strategy, and preparation to develop custom solutions designed to meet our clients' needs.

Most of our clients are entrepreneurs who do business on both sides of the border. Because their tax obligations are complex, we tirelessly scrutinize not only the Canadian tax laws, but US tax laws too. We make sure clients comply with the laws of both nations.

And we're not a hired gun. We don't just help them with their taxes and go home. Our clients value our opinion, and we strive to become a valuable part of their team.

We want to establish long-term relationships. We want to make a significant impact on their overall net worth so they can achieve their goals.

Our clients' financial health, both in the present and the future, is what matters most to us, so we do more than just their taxes. We also provide overall estate planning to ensure that their assets go to their successors in a tax-efficient manner.

When our clients call, we make sure they don't sit on hold listening to elevator music while waiting to hear a human voice on the other end. We know that's important because we're entrepreneurs, just like them.

We deliver personalized service with quick response times because their time is valuable. Time is money.

———————

In a better world, fewer people would need advice and assistance to comply with our nation's tax laws.

Businesses and entrepreneurs that pay employees, provide services, and generate income in Canada—and possibly in the US as well—will always need the guidance and assistance that a firm such as mine provides. But there's really no reason why average people who get a regular paycheck should have such a hard time figuring out how much they owe in taxes.

Why should they have to pay an accountant or a small accounting firm or a tax preparation conglomerate like H&R Block to do their taxes? Why should they have to buy tax software, sit down, and fill in all the program's blanks just to figure out what they owe the government? (And after all that, they still don't truly understand why they owe or pay the amount they do.)

Why should they view the thirtieth day of April with such fear and loathing?

And why do all of us take this for granted? Why is this our "normal"?

Why, indeed. It shouldn't be this way. It doesn't *have* to be this way.

It won't be easy to rewrite our tax statutes. It'll take years of hard work to design a simpler and fairer system than the one we've been tinkering with for the last half century—and even more years to make it law.

It'll take smart people who understand that you can't keep raising the income tax on the wealthy because we're already at the point where taxing them further will make them less inclined to work hard to make more money.

It'll take economists, academics, practitioners, and politicians who are willing to consider the pros and cons of implementing alternatives, such as a consumption tax to supplement or even replace the income tax.

I think that's a good idea. Others think it's a terrible idea. But one way or another, it's time to sit down and talk about it.

It won't be easy, and it won't be popular.

It will take guts.

I'd like to believe we have them.

Manufactured by Amazon.ca
Acheson, AB